Women Who Rock

Inspirational Stories of Success by Extraordinary Women

Natasha Duswalt

Hybrid Global Publishing

Published by
Hybrid Global Publishing
301 E 57th Street, 4th fl
New York, NY 10022

Manufactured in the United States of America, or in the United Kingdom when distributed elsewhere.

Author Duswalt, Natasha
    Women Who Rock
    Paperback: 9781938015656
    eBook: 9781938015663

Cover design by: Joe Potter
Cover Photoshop work by: Val Westover
Interior design: Scribe
Editing by: Ayse Yilmaz

www.NatashaDuswalt.com
www.PeakModels.com

AUTHOR PHOTOGRAPHERS

Natasha Duswalt—Val Westover
Dr. Barbara De Angelis—Charles Bush
Lisa Sasevich—Stacey Canfield
Isabel De Los Rios—Tony Morgan
Shanda Sumpter—Nikki Incandela
Karen Strauss—Stephanie Westover
Maryann Ehmann—Barbie Santos
Janie Lidey—Val Westover
Stephanie Adriana Westover—Val Westover
Lesley Nardini—Val Westover
Naomi Carmona-Morshead—Lisa Brook King
Robin deGroot—Val Westover
Mary Beth Gilbert—Deidhra Fahey
Bonnie Kitahata—Val Westover
Linda Kruse—Cutter Cutshaw
Lynette Louise—Tim Hale
Ellen Marrs—Brittany Carrillo
Debbie McCormick—Stephanie Westover
Siobhan McKenna—Kevin Connors
Kathy Pendleton—Mary Ann Halpin
Roberta Perry—Roberta Perry
B Heather Pinard—Val Westover
Diane Polnow—Ray Bengston
Veronica Centasso Pranzo—Val Westover
Neecol Resnin—Stephanie Westover
Barbara Starley—Elaine Kessler
Francine Tone—Jill Fleming
Tesy Ward—Vincent Innocente
Lori Zapata—Lori Zapata

DEDICATION

This book is dedicated to my true loves…
Craig, Tyler, Ryan and Hayden.
To my parents and grandparents who gave me my foundation.
To my sister Tania, brother Alex, Cameron, Cory, Tricia, Ron.
To Anne and Anton Duswalt, Pamela, William,
Courtney, Ashley, Taylor, Michael.
Thank you for lighting up my life!

This book is for those who live their lives
in pursuit of a higher purpose.

To those that realize that there is greatness
within each and every person.

Your life is a masterpiece—now go out
and make that your reality!

CONTENTS

INTRODUCTION

Women Who Rock is a collection of stories gathered from women from all walks of life. Each author who shares their story also reveals their unique female experience. We as the readers are pulled into their lives with a new appreciation and understanding of their journey.

With every story we can all find ourselves in a version of each author. The stories differ, the settings differ, but the need for the human spirit to triumph comes through loud and clear.

There is an unseen thread that within each story is the need and desire to move forward while taking along the lessons learned and insights gained. Women Who Rock sets the stage for women all over the world to look within and find their inner strength to live out their destiny. The purpose of this book is to lift others and show what is possible. Every author in this book started somewhere and has created a life of purpose. When one succeeds it gives everyone else the chance to succeed as well.

Women have the unique ability to bring life into the world, and with that honor comes great responsibility. I am honored at the thought of the lives this book will touch. I am honored to know that with every woman who decides to live the best version of herself that there will be an unseen positive reaction in her home, her life and her community.

Every woman who has the courage to light the way for others, is also lighting the way for future generations beyond her lifetime.

Natasha Duswalt
Women Who Rock

Let Your Light Shine

By Natasha Duswalt

We all have our story. The story we have lived and the story we tell that is the summary or "golden nuggets" that we extract for efficiency. Perhaps to avoid the pain of the truth. Perhaps it is a version of the story that seems more palatable to those around us. Perhaps our truth is too much to bear based on the fact that no one else seems to have a story that resembles anything we have endured.

I grew up in sunny California. The picture included Mom, Dad, older brother, and older sister in a lovely quiet, nice suburban neighborhood. The family was complete with the baby girl . . . me. From the moment I was able to comprehend what was around me, I was keenly aware that there was strife and conflict at all times. My family, although normal looking on the outside, was riddled with an addiction that pierced the very fabric of our lives. Our father who was a brilliant engineer also suffered greatly with alcohol addiction. Our lives from the early years were lived in fear and hiding. My sister, Tania, and brother, Alex, became my fierce protectors. They needed protecting as well but being the youngest I did not realize any of that at the time. Our amazing mother who struggled to keep us safe also put herself in danger on a regular basis to protect her children.

Some of my early memories included hiding in closets and cupboards to avoid being seen by our father when he was under the influence. When he was not under the influence, my father was a funny, kind, and loving person. This also made it all the more confusing. With his addiction in full swing, there was no sense of safety in our home. We later found out that his addiction may have been triggered by a brain tumor. Either way, the fallout of his behavior was devastating for our entire family.

There is no easy way as a child to understand why there is no food, and why you go to bed without dinner on some nights. There is no way to process that eating the stale box of old crackers that you were elated to find was going to, one day, shape you into an efficient person who truly understands what it is to be hungry. There is no way to realize when you are a little kid, picking fruit from the trees in the neighborhood just to have food, is not what the other kids were doing. To this day I love oranges and plums because they remind me of the fact that there was a divine plan to keep me alive even when all the odds were against me.

There is no understanding why your father is not like the other dads. There is no way to tell your mom when she leaves the house that he is going to lock me in the closet until she gets home. I could not tell her because he would say that if I did I would be in more trouble and so would my dog. At the age of about 5 years old I remember that closet so clearly—the darkness all around and the light coming through the crack at the bottom of the door. I would focus on the light.

As a small child, I did not understand why I was locked in the closet for what seemed to be an eternity. I just knew that with all of the darkness around me that my choice would be to focus on the light so that I would not be afraid. With only my eyes fixed on the light and my ability to hear sounds in the house I would wait to hear my mother's car pull up. It was then, I knew my sentence was lifted.

One day my mother realized that we had endured enough. My parents divorced and where most kids would be saddened, I felt a relief. I felt the freedom in knowing that it would just be us—my mom, my sister, and my brother. There was such a sense of peace and harmony. But that was short-lived—my mother met her second husband who invaded our lives and took our mother away.

Within a couple of years, she was remarried and this much-older-man took all of her time. She worked with him daily at his business. Our lives changed and within a year they were married.

My mother had not been home to Germany since she was 18 years old. She longed to see her father and that year her new husband took her on a trip to see her father in Germany. Twenty years had passed. I was the only sibling taken on the trip probably because I was the youngest and had never been away from my mother.

It was the summer of 1976. I was about to celebrate my 10th birthday in Germany and I would be meeting my grandfather for the first time.

My mother was elated, but she was also feeling that she needed to look like she did when she left Germany at 18 years old. So she dieted, excessively. She took diet pills, and she was so over-stimulated from the diet pills that even I, a nine-year-old child, could not keep up with her pace.

On my 10th birthday, my mom and I feel asleep in the guest bedroom. On that fateful night I would forever be changed as my mother suffered a massive heart attack in her father's house. I woke up suddenly, and tried desperately to wake her with no results. I did everything. I shook her, begged, and pleaded with her not to leave me, but it was done. She was gone. And in that moment, I knew I was alone.

My journey back the United States with the stranger my mother married was robotic at best. I was devastated, numb, and did not speak unless it was completely necessary. I arrived back to the U.S. and soon was told that there was "good news"—my father would be back to take care of my sister, brother. and me. This was far from good news for any of us. Within days, our lives spiraled out of control. His grief turned into the inability to care for anyone—not even himself.

It was so bad living with my father, I was advised by my grandmother to write a letter to the district attorney to ask for help. After my letter was answered, there were a few follow-up discussions which culminated with me taking my father to court to ask a judge to be removed from his care.

There are very few things that scare me but that day I was terrified to face my father and tell the judge that we had no milk, no bread, and to tell him that I would routinely walk out of school because I knew that there was no one going to stop me. I had become an adult at the age of eleven. I was making adult decisions to save my own life. Those decisions resulted in me being placed in a tempo-rary foster situation with my mother's friend who took me in for the year until my grandmother could make arrangements to move from Michigan and come back to California to care for me.

I spent the next few years immersed in school. I knew my life was different from the other kids. It always had been that way. I wanted that to change. I wanted to be normal. I decided to focus on the good. I took the qualities I loved in my mother and mir-rored them. I took her kindness, her empathy, her compassion and I decided that those would be my traits as well. I excelled in everything I focused on. I was able to get out of school one year early and tested out in the 97th percentile. I loved school but also was bored easily if I was not challenged.

My grandmother provided a solid routine and disciplined life that I was not accustomed to in my early years. Her old school Russian routines were very grounded in love, respect, and doing the right thing. She was all that was right in this world. She did the right thing even when it was not popular. She was the beacon of light that my life needed. At 17 years old I left my grandmother to embark on my adult journey and discovery of who I would become.

I met a hairdresser and asked her if I could model in a runway show at the age of 17 and suddenly I had a job in an industry I found exciting. Take note that I ASKED if I could do the show—I was not paid, I just did it to get the experience. This is a major shift in the way people do things. We are all looking for the big pay day—sometimes you have to do something just so you can get in the door!

I went to college for a short period but found that I could not keep up financially while attending. I had a few jobs here and there but modeling was much more lucrative. I was at the point in my life financially where I would only be able to afford a Reese's Peanut Butter Cup for dinner, where I would have $2.00 for gas for the week to get to a restaurant job that I was eventually fired from for not being able to open champagne bottles. All of this was so ridiculous but at the time it was also devastating. I was broke and hungry, and did not have a place to call home. I was basically couch surfing while I figured out this thing called life.

Once I started booking modeling jobs my life became an adventure. I traveled around the world modeling for designers and clothing companies from NY to Miami to Mexico to Hong Kong, Japan, Taiwan, and all over the Los Angeles market. I was disciplined where others were not. I showed up because I saw the opportunities disguised as hard work. I took the jobs no one else wanted to do. The low paying fashion show for one company only paying $50.00 with one hundred dress changes. I also took the seasonal swim shows in New York City when no one was hiring in Los Angeles. Heck, I got a trip and a paycheck! Other models laughed at me because they thought it was weird that I would travel across country for an opportunity to work for only a couple of days. They did not realize that a job where there were bagels available to a gal that was eating Reese's Peanut Butter Cups for dinner was a perk! I used to think, "So I am getting paid to work AND they have bagels? Win, win!" And let's not forget that at the end of the day they are going to toss the leftovers. Dinner is served.

Again opportunity is not always dressed up in the easy package. Sometimes it is the hard things that lead to the bigger prizes. I did not have anyone back home to take care of me. I was it. I was all I had and I had to rely on my skills and abilities. I was a hard worker and that never failed me. I had to make it. Hunger is a great motivator!

So with a modeling career in full swing, I was still the same little girl on the inside that did not know my worth. When you grow up in danger, you get a sense that your value is lower because if you had any value, these things would not be happening. This type of thinking can cloud anyone's perceptions. I was prone to dating men that were not good for me in the long run. I seemed to actually find the guys that mirrored my father's worst traits. Once I was aware of that fact, I was able to stop that pattern and truly find the people that would be supportive and loving.

After a few failed relationships, I took a year to figure out who I was. I declined all dates and spent that time working on my inner self. I knew that the answers were within and I just needed to access my own personal power. I realized that my life was shaped in faith even when I had no faith. Looking at life in reverse shows you where you were never alone and that your faith was always there you just did not see it. I was able to find out my true self, which led me to creating a list of things I truly wanted in my life. I wrote down my goals and dreams. Some seemed out of reach others seemed silly. I still wrote them down.

With the year of writing down my dreams and goals I met my husband, Craig. If you know Craig, you know that I found a bright light and probably the most motivated, hard-working, kind, and loving person who would do anything for anyone.

It's possible. There are great people out there! I was able to find someone who shared the same values, and who wanted the same things. We were able to create a life of purpose. I was able to start my company Peak Models & Talent with cheap letterhead and plain business cards, along with a ton of passion and drive.

I was excited that I was able to overcome my fears to create an agency where models could book work without compromising their values in a business where a lot of "interesting" options are out there. Peak Models & Talent was created to be a bright light in a business that can often be tainted with some unsafe situations. We wanted to take that out of the equation. The company grew faster than we could keep up.

We both wanted kids. We both wanted freedom to be with our kids and still run our businesses. This all seemed impossible but I am here to tell you that it is all more than possible, because we did it.

Our three boys were born and our lives took on a whole other level of busy. We had a shared vision of being able to raise our boys with both of us 100% available.

With Peak Models & Talent established in Los Angeles, we focused on our staff and our family and everything was going as planned. But remember opportunities show up sometimes dressed in unappealing packages. We were getting one of those packages.

An opportunity showed up that would forever change the course of our lives. I was diagnosed with Hodgkin's Lymphoma cancer.

Our kids were 1, 3, and 5, and our world was now turned upside down. I did not want this delivery. I had no intention of owning this diagnosis. I had to deal with this mess and I would but I knew in my head I was NOT owning it.

In my opinion this was a temporary setback, or better yet it was a SET UP for something more. I was not going to stay in the diagnosis. I was going to get the medical treatments and I was going to move on with my life.

The truth is that everyone has something. My story revealed to me that we are not *defined by our past, we are prepared by our past.*

I had endured great fear in the past. I had been surrounded by darkness and I looked to the light and kept my focus there. I am also reminded when I tell my story that I do not have anything figured out and that I am still learning and growing. I may have some experience in some arenas that may help someone else and if that is the case I am honored to be of service.

The same thing holds true for cancer, for any heartbreak, for starting a business, for any new venture. There is a complete surrender and an understanding that we cannot do this thing called life alone. We need to focus on the light, to help each other and lift each other up. There is simply so much we can do if we just realize that we are more capable than we think, we can endure more than we know, and that we are more powerful than we have ever imagined.

We can lift people up with our words. We can light the way for another just with our story. When one person triumphs in *any way,* it gives everyone else hope and permission to do the same in their life.

We are here to help each other. If a girl who had no help in this world other than a will and a drive to succeed can create a business without the usual college degree, rise out of poverty and overcome cancer, just imagine what you can do! The only limits we have are the limits we believe.

Focus your eyes on the light and make your life the masterpiece it was meant to be.

Natasha Duswalt is an author, speaker, and the president and founder of Peak Models & Talent in Los Angeles. As an international model, Natasha has had the rare opportunity to travel all over the world in places including New York, Miami, Hong Kong, Japan, Taiwan, Mexico and several other locations working with top designers and companies. Natasha has been featured on numerous television shows including Baywatch and Growing Pains, as well as the hit movie by Oliver Stone, "The Doors." She was also hired as an ESPN Spokesmodel and has appeared on numerous television commercials.

Peak Models & Talent has been touted as one of Los Angeles' top agencies, booking with high-end clients such as Guess, Forever 21, Six Flags Theme Parks, Kardashians, Kendall & Kylie, Intel, Nokia, Reebok, Disney, ABS Clothing, Skechers, Nike, Dell, Audi, Mercedes, Honda, Speedo, Tempurpedic Sleep Systems, Starbucks, Bebe, Wells Fargo, Honda, Patagonia, Princess Cruises, Tommy Bahama, Kmart and Target just to name a few.

Natasha, a proud cancer survivor, currently lives in Los Angeles with her husband, Craig Duswalt, and their three boys.

For speaking inquiries please email Natasha@craigduswalt.com or Natasha@peakmodels.com.

www.NatashaDuswalt.com

Honoring My Soul Accomplishments

By Barbara De Angelis Ph.D.

I remember at the end of my last year in High School, those of us in the graduating class of 1969 were asked to choose a goal we wanted to achieve. The list was published for everyone to see. Most of the items were predictable: Become a doctor; get married and have two children; own my own business; become a professional tennis player; move to California; buy a home in Florida; get elected to public office.

My contribution to the list was: *Be Free.*

At the time, I wasn't even sure what it meant to be free, but I knew it was what I wanted. There were no self-help books in those days, no motivational TV programs or transformational seminars. *'Living as an awakened human'* wasn't on a list of possible career paths from which we could choose, but it was the only one that interested me. (Fortunately, I soon found a teacher who helped me become successful at my chosen vocation!)

If most people were asked to make a list of the things they wanted to accomplish in their lifetime, *"To truly know myself"* would most likely not be near the top of their list, or even on the list. For a seeker of truth, however, that accomplishment becomes one of the most treasured attainments we would ever hope to achieve. It is what I call *a Soul Accomplishment.*

I recall being included on another list: The names of students who were voted *"Most Likely to Succeed."* Naturally by 'succeed', my classmates meant be known for something and make money at something—external goals. Looking back, I realize that even something as innocuous as entries in a high school yearbook programs us to define success in a particular way.

We live in a society focused on external accomplishments. When someone tells us they have a friend we should meet, one of the first questions we ask is, "What does he do?" or "What's her background?" When we evaluate others, or ourselves, it's usually based on how much external success we've achieved, how much money we have, how we look, and what we've acquired.

Nothing's wrong with outer achievements. I have earned many of them—I've written 16 bestselling books that have been read by tens of millions of people, hosted my own TV shows, been awarded the highest honor as an inspirational speaker, and much more. **However, our material goals become a problem if they overshadow the quest for our Soul Goals,** *those inner attainments that aren't about achievement or acquisition, but about true mastery.*

Every day, I see wonderful, conscious people who've attained great personal mastery, yet who suffer and condemn themselves because they don't feel successful, all because their achievements don't fit the picture of how they think success is *supposed* to look. They're living lives of authenticity, compassion, service, humility, gratitude, and grace. All of these are astonishing Soul Accomplishments, but since they can't be measured or valued in traditional terms—money, prestige, possessions—they're discounted.

What if, from the Highest vantage point of Consciousness, the purpose of your journey is not for you to become anything, get anything, or acquire anything, but to remember and live as who you truly are—an individual expression of great Light and great Love?

What if you are here to gather and acquire the wisdom that will elevate and uplift your Soul, so that each day you can say, *"I'm wiser than I was yesterday. I see more clearly than I saw yesterday. I understand more than I understood yesterday."*

What if your true accomplishments happen in your character, in your heart, and in your soul, and cannot be measured by the limited constructs of the world?

What if your Success Goal every day was the following:

**Today I want to live as the most awakened,
loving human being I can.
I want to stay awake
and be more awake at the end of the day
than I was when the day began.**

**What are Soul Accomplishments? They are those things that
nothing and no one can ever take away from you.** You've made
great Soul Accomplishments if you can say any of the following:

*Today I thought deeply about things.
I realized I was shutting off, and reached out to reconnect.
I forgave myself instead of beating myself up.
I lightened up about something.
I had compassion for someone I would have judged.
I chose the Highest thought and shifted my attitude about an issue.
I loved myself even though I wasn't perfect.
I remembered to be grateful for being alive.
I was conscious.
I did not go back to sleep.*

These are Soul Accomplishments. The other things that occurred
on the outside are just the events of the day. One day you make
more money, one day you make less money. One day your day at
work is calm, one day it's chaotic. One day your home life is peace-
ful, one day it's contentious. If you evaluate your success based
on those ever-changing external circumstances, you'll be setting
yourself up for unhappiness.

This is exactly how we often sabotage our feeling of accomplishment: **we believe that to feel good about ourselves means we
need *more* of something. We have to get more, or do more, and
when we don't, we conclude that we've failed.**

There's nothing wrong with wanting "more" except that we're
usually focusing on more of the wrong things rather than those

qualities and choices that would bring us closer to our Highest. *And for me, my commitment has always been to become more on the inside rather than only trying to get more and do more on the outside.*

Is there really a way to be more without getting more? Of course there is! Every day you *can* be more. You may not be able to acquire more, or do more but you can always be more. *That's because true Soul Accomplishments don't depend on anyone else but you.*

**'More' has to start inside of you.
You can be more giving; you can be more compassionate;
you can be more forgiving; you can be more grateful;
you can be more courageous; you can be more loving.**

For me, being a transformational teacher has always been and continues to be a sacred experience. When I see people looking into the depth of their heart, and staring down their patterns and their masks with the eyes of truth, it gives me hope for humanity. So few people actually choose to do this when they're alive. To see yourself, the darkness and the light, and to shift and shift—these are great Soul Accomplishments for which you deserve to be honored.

I call this 'seeing yourself through God's eyes,' or Spirit's eyes. Do you really think that some great Cosmic Being or Intelligence, whatever you imagine it is, would say, *"You know, I don't think those sales numbers are really good. Hmmm, she didn't close that deal today. Did I see her eating two portions of ice cream? What about that cellulite—that's unattractive. What a messy desk—that certainly doesn't present a good case for her Soul. No, I don't think she's doing that well."*

This imaginary scenario should help you see the absurdity of how much you beat yourself up for simply being human. Naturally, the thought of a Higher Power judging you as a failure because of the things for which you judge yourself is ridiculous—but so is your habit of disqualifying your Soul Accomplishments.

One of the "Soul Shift Practices" I suggest you try is *making a list of your Soul Accomplishments.* I use this practice all the time. This is a powerful exercise that will create an immediate shift as you look at yourself through the eyes of Spirit, rather than the eyes of your parents, or your competitive best friend from college, or your nemesis at work, or your critics, real or imaginary. This isn't something to do in one sitting and then conclude that you're finished. Noticing your Soul Accomplishments should be an ongoing process and an ever present part of your life.

Here are some of my personal Soul Accomplishments:

- Keeping my heart fully open to the fullness of loving no matter how many times I have been hurt or had to let go of a dream, and never shutting down or shutting off for one moment of my life.
- Teaching from a place of hope, inspiration, and complete dedication even during times in when I was personally experiencing despair and loss.
- Having the tenacity, patience, and fortitude to stand by something or someone even with no immediate reward or progress, and not let go of my conviction that it was the right thing to do.
- Never fostering friendships with others in my industry because of what I could get from knowing them, or how the connection could benefit me, and insisting on only having authentic relationships founded in integrity.
- Knowing when it was time to help both of my dogs leave their bodies and go forward on their journey, even though I wanted to hold on.
- Turning down opportunities for more fame or fortune when the projects were not in alignment with the Highest for me, even though it meant having less income and a much less glamorous lifestyle than most of my colleagues.
- Giving myself time and space to go through profound rebirth several times in my life rather than pushing myself to write a book every year in order to be commercially successful, and instead, waiting for right moment to birth new wisdom.
- Learning how, when it was necessary, to let go of situations, people and attachments in every area of my life, and move forward without looking back.

- Never giving anything less than 100% effort, even when no one else is watching, and always approaching everything with the utmost of sincerity.
- Being willing to share this list with you.

Right now, if nothing else ever changed in your life, you have many Soul Accomplishments for which to honor yourself. Honor yourself for the choice to be awake and conscious. Honor yourself for the choice to open, to feel, to see, and to shift. Honor yourself for the ways in which you've served and loved others. Honor yourself for your moments of revelation and humility. Honor yourself for reading this book, and every book you've ever read to guide you on your path to freedom.

Dr. Barbara De Angelis is one of the most influential teachers of our time in the field of personal and spiritual transformation. As a renowned author, speaker, and media personality for more than four decades, she's reached tens of millions of people with her inspirational messages about how to create a life of freedom, mastery, and awakening. Barbara has written 16 best-selling books that have sold over 10 million copies including four #1 New York Times *bestsellers. Among her popular titles are* Soul Shifts; Real Moments; *and her most recent book* The Choice for Love: Entering Into a New, Enlightened Relationship with Yourself, Others and the World.

www.barbaradeangelis.com

A Rocker Chick's Experience in the Denim Business

By Daniella Clarke

I spent most of my early twenties on the side of a stage watching my husband, Gilby Clarke, play guitar for the world's biggest rock band, Guns N' Roses. We toured the world and had adventures that most people could only dream about, but the greatest adventure of my life came when I went into business.

I started to make jeans for my girlfriends and myself. I had always altered and made my own clothes—when I was twelve, my mom bought me a sewing machine which opened up a whole new world for me. I loved to make clothes for myself. I used to raid her linen closet for fabric; I would use Rid Dye in the bathtub to dye her sheets into a fun color, then I would cut and sew myself a skirt or a dress. I pretty much spent every free moment I had dreaming up a new outfit for myself, and as I got older, I would do it as I listened to all the music that inspired me.

My mom used to get so upset when she would search her closet for a beautiful sequin dress, only to find it in my sewing machine . . . except I had turned it into a jacket. I always had a very strong passion for fashion.

As it was, I was watching an old Woodstock documentary and really loved how the hippies were wearing their jeans so low on the hip. Then I saw a picture of Robert Plant from Led Zeppelin standing in front of an airplane in the sexiest jeans ever! That's it! I thought. I'm making myself a pair of sexy super low-rise jeans.

Every girl knows that the one thing that's worse than shopping for a bathing suit is shopping for a pair of jeans. They never fit right and they always make your ass look like hell. I wanted jeans that looked like they were made especially for my body. I wanted them to be low and sexy on my hip and fitted through my thigh with a slight flare to balance out my shape.

Little did I know that I had found a huge gaping hole in the market place! The jeans I wanted did not exist. I started by buying old Levi's that were too big in the waist. I would take them home, rip them apart in the inner seam, lower the rise, and take in the thigh by re-cutting and taking away a couple of inches. I would sew them back up and voila! I did this for a while and wore them around town and on tour with Gilby. Soon, I was making them for Gilby and some of my girlfriends, and then his musician friends wanted a pair. I started to realize that I was getting a lot of attention for my jeans. I was constantly getting stopped in the streets, in nightclubs, malls; wherever I was, people would stop me and say, "Excuse me, where did you get your jeans?" And then my epiphany moment came: I was in the mall shopping, when an actress named Lara Flynn Boyle approached me.

"Excuse me, where can I get those jeans you are wearing?" I told her that I had made them. She said, "If I pay you, will you make me a pair? I have to have them!" I instantly knew that I could start a business by making and selling jeans.

Frankie was just starting preschool, so I would now have the time to start a little business for myself. I was over trying to keep myself busy by folding laundry, running the vacuum, doing dishes from breakfast, grocery shopping, and getting dinner going. I had been doing that for a few years and before that I was following Gilby on tour. It was my turn. I was twenty-nine.

I decided to use the money that I had earned from doing commercials to start my company. I had $5,000 left over. I didn't know much about the garment industry, but I approached it from a consumer's point of view. I knew where I shopped and what I would be willing to spend on a good fitting pair of jeans.

I started by going to downtown Los Angeles to the garment district to begin my research. I walked into a bookstore and purchased an industry newspaper called The Apparel News; I read the classified ads and found a pattern maker, label company, button company, zipper company, and a sewing contractor. I walked up and down the garment district and found lots of fabric shops that sold denim and I asked them where they bought the denim from directly. They gave me a few names of denim mills. I contacted the denim mills and arranged to purchase sample yardage of a dark indigo denim with 2% Lycra. I started off with 100 yards. It was important for me to have stretch in my fabric so the jeans could be skintight. I found a few factories in downtown Los Angeles and some in the surrounding cities. Looking back, I'm sure it probably was not very safe for a young woman to be walking around there alone and especially at night, but I was on a mission. Sometimes I would sit in my car for a few minutes just so I could assess the neighborhood and say a little prayer before I sprinted into the factory. I would ask God to please watch over me while I tried to have these jeans made.

One time, someone referred me to a sewing contractor in South L.A, a notoriously dicey neighborhood. I arranged for a meeting with the owner to schedule production of fifty pairs of jeans. The owner said it would take two weeks but I needed to pay upfront. I paid him and went home so excited. The next two weeks felt like a month. I couldn't wait to see my jeans all done up.

I called the contractor to make sure the jeans were done, but I got his voicemail. I left a message. After a few days passed and I hadn't heard back I called again and this time someone answered. When I asked to speak to the owner, I was told he was out of town and my production would not be done for an additional two weeks. I was so disappointed. After the next two weeks, passed I called and again I felt like I was getting the run around, so I decided to drive down to the factory. When I arrived one of the men working there told me to wait in an office while he went to get the owner. After waiting for about thirty minutes the door opened and four men walked in. They surrounded me. I thought, Well, this is it. I'm going to get beaten up or killed over jeans. I was terrified! The owner got in my face as the other men glared at all 105 pounds of me.

He asked, "What do you want?"

"I only came to pick up my jeans."

He started to yell at me, "I don't like your attitude and don't need you calling here asking if your jeans are ready. You get out of here!"

I was shocked. "But I paid you already!" He and his men said nothing else; they simply glared at me and walked out. I had been had! They had my jeans and they had my money.

I had to start all over again and I did. I found a little factory that had an ad in the Apparel News.

It was located in a city called Vernon, close to downtown. I made an appointment and went in for a meeting. A short Hispanic lady with curly red hair named Kuka met with me, and promised me a quick one-week turnaround for my fifty pairs of jeans. True to her word, exactly one week later my first production was ready. I named my denim line Frankie B. after my daughter.

Once my jeans were done I took them home in the back of my car to show Gilby. It felt so good to have them finished and I was so excited to see them go from an idea in my head to an actual product with a label on them.

Next came my list of things to do in order to launch the brand. I knew of a good photographer from my time in modeling. I gave him a call and asked him if he would take some pictures of me wearing the jeans. We shot some very sexy pictures in which I wore nothing but the jeans. I didn't want any distractions. I wanted the focus to be on the jeans.

After the shoot, I had my neighbors, a married couple who happened to be graphic designers, help me design my logo and put together a layout of the images we shot. I decided to make up post-cards with the picture of me wearing the jeans. I made a list of all the stores I wanted to be in.

The first one, and most important at the time, was Fred Segal on Melrose. I knew that they were a cutting-edge boutique and that stylists and celebrities shopped there. I also knew that it was a trend-setting store. I mailed the postcards out to my hit list of stores with a simple note saying, "Hi, I have a sexy new denim line called Frankie B. that I think would do great in your store. Please call me to set up an appointment to show you the line. Thanks, Daniella."

A week later, I drove to Fred Segal wearing my jeans and walked into their denim department. I wasn't twenty feet in before a sales girl stopped me and asked, "Excuse me, but who makes your jeans?" I replied with a very enthusiastic voice, "I do! They're called Frankie B." She looked me up and down and said, "Don't move. I'm going to fetch our buyer—I want him to see these." I waited.

I stood there, in the middle of the store, feeling like I might pee myself when the manager walked in.

He said right away, "Hey, are you the girl that sent me the postcard?"

I said that I was and he quickly continued, staring down at my hips, "Those are really low! I tell you what, I'm going to have my sales girls try them on and if they fit them, I will give them a try." I quickly ran to my car to get a couple pairs of jeans, all the while praying that the girls would fit into them. Luckily for me, they both loved them; they came out of the dressing room beaming with excitement. They looked great in the jeans. The buyer turned to me and said, "Great, I will take thirty pairs and see how they do."

I asked if he could please pay me cash on delivery because I needed the money to buy more fabric. He agreed, I gave him a small cash discount, and unloaded the jeans from the back of my car. That was on a Friday. Monday morning I received a call from him saying, "Daniella, we sold out of your jeans. I'll take fifty more." I was stunned! I ran into the living room and excitedly told Gilby the good news. This was great!

I knew how much weight Fred Segal carried with the other stores, so my plan was to let all them know that my jeans just sold out at there. I then walked into a store in the Beverly Center in Los Angeles, and amazingly, the same thing happened: The minute I walked through the door wearing my jeans a sales girl stopped me and said, "Where are those jeans that you're wearing from?" I told her the brand name and that they just sold out at Fred Segal. She said, "I'll take fifty pairs."

From then on, that was my sales line and everything snowballed from there. I didn't have a sales rep back then. I did it all myself. I was a one-woman show for my first year in business. I designed, manufactured, sold, and delivered the line. The first year I made about $50,000.00 in sales and I was thrilled. I never thought it would get that big. I just thought I could make some cute jeans that maybe other girls would like to wear and hopefully make a little extra money to help contribute to our household bills.

One day I was at the grocery store waiting in line when I saw a magazine called Detour with Meg Ryan on the cover. She looked so sexy, which was a real departure from her "America's Sweetheart" image. I looked to see who the photographer was—it was Herb Ritts. I threw the magazine in my cart and took it home to read it. As I was looking at the pictures of Meg Ryan, I noticed that there was a shot of her wearing a pair of low-slung sexy jeans. I could feel my blood pressure rising as I called out to Gilby to come have a look.

"Gilby, someone has already knocked off my jeans—look!"

Gilby scanned the image and said, "Daniella, did you not see the credits? They say jeans by Frankie B." I just about fell off the couch. I couldn't believe it! I found out later that the stylist for that shoot bought the jeans at Fred Segal.

The following year I sold $1.5 million; by the third year I sold $6.5 million, and by our sixth year we reached sales of $15 million. We were growing so fast, I felt like I was being carried by wild horses and I could barely hold on to the reins.

Daniella Clarke is a fashion visionary born of a rock 'n' roll fairy tale.

While on a family vacation in California, Daniella was walking down Hollywood's Walk of Fame when she met and fell in love with a local guitar player named Gilby Clarke.

Soon after, the couple hit the road with his band, Guns N' Roses. While on tour, Daniella was inspired to start designing after people kept asking about her one-of-a-kind jeans. She launched the Frankie B. brand, named after the couple's daughter Frankie in 1999.

As the founder and president of Frankie B., Daniella revolutionized the denim market, creating the instantly recognizable, low-rise silhouette that defined an era. She built an international brand around L.A.'s free-thinking, rocker-chic spirit, with one guiding design principle: "When you turn around and look in the mirror, you want a good view."

Jennifer Lopez wore the brand's jumpsuit on the cover of her 2001 album, "Love Don't Cost A Thing," which landed the label's name all over billboards in Times Square, and soon, Frankie B. became the go-to for women in Hollywood and beyond, including Kate Moss, Sienna Miller, Miley Cyrus, Kate Hudson, Megan Fox, Fergie, Katie Holmes, Jessica Alba, and many others.

Under Daniella's guidance, the brand grew into a lifestyle concept, generating more than $200 million in sales selling denim (more than 1.5 million pairs), tops, bottoms, dresses, active wear, and eyewear in 4,000 stores worldwide.

Daniella took part in Mercedes-Benz Fashion Week in Los Angeles, and was featured in Vogue, Glamour, Elle, People, In Style, Time, *and numerous other fashion and lifestyle publications. As a style expert, she appeared on* America's Next Top Model, Access Hollywood, Extra, E!, *and* CNN.

She was a leader in reviving the denim industry in Southern California, and elevating the market as a destination for premium products and trends. In 2004, Daniella was awarded the MAFI Fashion Innovator of the Year award for her contributions, and three years later she was honored with a Media Award from Y-ME National Breast Cancer Organization for her support and dedication to the charity.

After selling Frankie B. in 2011, she embarks on the next chapter of the fairytale with Weslin + Grant. Daniella launched her new brand in 2016, naming it after two sentimental Southern California addresses. Grant is the street where she and Gilby first lived in Los Angeles, and Weslin is the one where they had their daughter Frankie, now 21.

The collection marks an evolution for the designer with a focus on effortless and understated essentials with a modern edge. The pieces have enough versatility to go from a relaxed, 'what? I woke up this way' look, to rock show-ready with the toss of a blazer. "I was inspired by 70's silhouettes and images of Lauren Hutton in those great androgynous suits from that time. We now live in an age where women are as powerful as men and I wanted this collection to embody that. Weslin + Grant is for the woman that doesn't need to be told how to wear it because she instinctually knows what to do!" Standout styles include buttery-soft, slouchy leather blazers and trousers, skinny velveteen corduroy suits and denim moto vests. Look for the collection to hit stores in the Fall of 2016.

www.WeslinAndGrant.com

How I Discovered My Million Dollar Value

By Lisa Sasevich

It was about 10 years ago and my 40th birthday was in view. I felt grateful to be doing work that I loved. I had a 2 year old and could feel the spirit of my next baby asking to be birthed. My then-husband was in his umpteenth year of training to become a heart-surgeon. Life was good. . . . and busy!

Because I loved my work so much, the hours and days passed quickly. I was working for a small seminar company that was teaching women how to create powerful partnerships with the men in their lives. I did their weekend seminar and it changed my life, and it was such an honor to now be leading the charge on the growth of that company as their Director of Marketing Monday through Friday and workshop leader on the weekends.

And then it all came to screeching halt. To my surprise, I was fired from my dream job the night before Christmas Eve. The explanation I was given made no sense until years later when I became the CEO of my own multi-million dollar company.

I later found out that the owner told one of her students that she let me go because I was a star, and there was no room for stars in that company. The truth is, that wouldn't have made sense to me at the time but now I see that letting me go was the biggest gift that God, the Universe, and my boss at the time could have given me in my life.

It forced me onto a journey of exploration. It forced me to ask the hard questions. It forced me to discover what I now call my blessings. . . . my Million Dollar Value.

And in that I've come to see that each and every one of us has a Million Dollar Value; a blessing, a gift, some innate talent, or hard earned expertise that is ours to bring to the world. Every one of us has that nagging feeling inside that we were meant for more. . . . And I'm here to tell you, it's true!

After I was fired, while in the pain of that shock and disbelief, I hired a coach to help me get some clarity on my next steps. I had to do something to figure out how to turn these lemons into lemonade and to support my family. The coach asked me what kind of things I loved to do. What came naturally to me that was difficult for others? What lit me up and made me feel passionate?

I felt kind of shallow that so much of what came to my mind was associated with the work I had been doing, but since it was all I could think of, I shared it anyway. I told him how much it lit me up when I would lead introductory evenings to introduce women to our seminars and 30, 50, 60% of them would register on-the-spot for our $400 weekend workshop. And how my heart would leap out of my chest when at that first weekend, when I got the chance to tell them about our three other workshops and make them a really irresistible offer if they registered for one, two, or all three that night, and up to 80% of them would say YES and register!

I went on to share how obsessed I had become with figuring out how to make that happen again and again. How to give people what they need to say yes on-the-spot, and how it wasn't even about them saying yes to me . . . it was about them saying yes to themselves through me.

I experimented with everything from how to set the chairs, how much content to teach, which content to teach, should I take questions? Should I let them share or not? How do I make a safe container for people to learn alongside of strangers? What should my pricing be? Should I offer payment plans? Bonuses? End late? End early? And so on. . . .

At some point, he interrupted me and said, "Lisa, are you seriously confused about your Million Dollar Value?"

I guess I was so close to it, I couldn't see it. Kind of like the tip of your nose; you know it's there and you can feel how close it is, but you truly can't see it!

He went on to tell me that having 30–80% of an audience say Yes and make an investment on-the-spot was almost unheard of. He shared that there was a huge market of mission-driven, heart-centered people like me who would give their left arm to learn to do this so they could help more people. To sell, without being pushy or salesy.

The truth is, I had never seen it that way until he said it. I was in my own bubble. I just wanted other women to have the amazing experience I had in those workshops and I knew that if they didn't register the night they came to the intro event, or on the phone call we would have when they called to find out more, that the odds are, they would never register and would never get to experience the awesome relationships I had learned to create from those workshops.

And that's how I discovered my blessings which eventually turned into my brand, The Invisible Close, and all of amazing online and live training that you can learn more about at: www.LisaSasevich.com

I'm here to tell you that we all have a Million Dollar Value. Sometimes we tuck it away because we tried giving it to someone who didn't value it and they made us feel small. Or we know it's there but we don't know how to talk about it. Or because it comes so easy to us, we don't realize how game changing it would be for another person to learn our system, our method, our mindset, and our practices in that area.

Did I always feel like a woman who rocks? The truth is, I always suspected she was inside me, and I bet you do too. I hope you'll use this story to tap into your own blessing. What's on the tip of your nose that you just can't see . . . yet!

Ranked on the prestigious Inc. 500/5000 list of America's Fastest Growing Private Companies for 2 years in a row, **Lisa Sasevich** **"The Queen of Sales Conversion"** *teaches experts who are making*

a difference how to get their message out and enjoy massive results, **without being "salesy."** *After 25 years of winning Top Sales Awards and training senior executives at companies like Pfizer and Hewlett-Packard, she left corporate America and put her skills to the test delivering high-impact sales-closing strategies for turbo-charging entrepreneurs and small business owners to great profits. In just a few short years,* **Lisa created a multi-million dollar home-based business** *with two toddlers in tow. Lisa really is the undisputed expert on how to make BIG money doing what you love!*

www.LisaSasevich.com

The Freedom of Success

By Isabel De Los Rios

It hit me like a ton of bricks . . ."Is this really happening?"

Often we hear stories about how quickly bad things come to strike us, but in this case, it was the complete opposite . . . the awesomeness of the moment hit me like a Mack truck, literally stopping me in my mommy tracks.

It was a cold, beautifully sunny day in Chicago. We woke up early in our small, one-bedroom hotel room, and before 9 am all four of us were ready to go. My kiddos, Christian (7) and Marcos (5), didn't usually hustle this fast in the morning, but on this particular day, we were going on a long-awaited visit to the Museum of Science and Industry, a place they had picked out based on pictures they'd seen on the internet.

Was it a vacation? Was it a school field trip? Well, it was kind of both! That past summer my husband, Stewart, and I had decided to homeschool our 2 young boys, so I guess you could say it was a vacation and school all rolled into one.

Several months prior, making the decision to homeschool wasn't an easy one, although it was something both of us really wanted. I was currently working full-time and Stewart was also working, as well as being volunteer football coach at our local high school. Our schedules didn't exactly leave much room for taking over what are some of the most important foundational school years in a child's life.

But the decision was almost made "for us" when we realized that Christian (6 years old at the time) was really struggling with school in many ways. He was having difficulty completing his schoolwork, and his behavior was less than stellar (to put it lightly). We knew something needed to change; something had to be done, but we didn't know what.

"Let's homeschool the boys ourselves" my husband said. At the time, the kids were being taught by a wonderful teacher in our home. As great as she was, Christian was acting out in so many ways that communicated to us, "Mommy and Daddy, I need YOU."

It was a leap of faith in every way, but we decided to give this homeschool thing the old college try. Stewart kept his volunteer position but stopped working so that he could take over teaching the boys while I continued to work full-time.

But how could we so easily make the decision for Stewart to stop working? I know for many families a quick decision like that is not really an option.

Well, for us, it was many years in the making.

Nine years prior, before two kids were even a thought in our minds, my husband and I had decided we were going to create an online business and sell a nutrition manual I had created called "The Diet Solution Program" to the world. The truth is, we were clueless, not even knowing where to begin. Nor did we know the amount of work it was going to take to make this online business a reality, but we'd seen so many other people "making money online" and were determined to figure out what that meant.

Well, the story of how "The Diet Solution Program" turned into what is known today as "Beyond Diet," and went from selling 2 books a day to having sold hundreds of thousands of books worldwide over the past 9 years could be an entire book in itself, filled with high points, low points, hardships, and wonderful moments combined. But most importantly, the business ended up providing things to my husband and I that we had no idea we would now be enjoying.

First, we were able to run our business from anywhere in the country, as long as we had internet. We knew this would be the case, but we did not realize the magnitude of how this would affect our lives in a positive way until we were able to leave our tiny apartment in cold New Jersey and relocate to a lovely, spacious home in sunny and beautiful South Carolina. Not only is the weather pretty incredible, but we're now able to raise our children much closer to their grandparents, one of the greatest blessings in my family's life.

Another incredible benefit of our business is that it enabled Stewart to leave behind the long, draining hours of work in corporate America, and he can now be home more with our boys. No longer did he have to leave home before 7 am and return after 7 pm, but could now be home to see both boys take their first steps, say their first words, and see their smiling faces when he woke up every morning.

And then there were the travel perks, as was the case on that beautiful morning in Chicago. Having a business that only requires a computer and internet allowed for us to not only take the trip described above, but hundreds of incredible trips. From Hawaii, Mexico, and the Bahamas, to California, Arizona, and Colorado (the list is long) . . . over the past 9 years, these trips are something that without the business, we'd never have been able to experience.

There were many moments over the course of the past 9 years that have felt "successful" to me; purchasing our lakeside home in South Carolina, buying our first fancy car, and flying first-class for the first time. But none of those moments quite compared to the overwhelming gratitude I felt flooding me in the hotel room that morning.

What was it about this particular instance that felt like such overwhelming success to me?

It was the freedom to be with my family and to teach my boys exactly as I wanted without inhibition. That level of freedom, to me, felt better than any car, any home, or any amount of "stuff" money could ever buy.

Success is often measured in things we can see . . . the dollar amount in our bank accounts, the price of our flashy car, or the price tag on all the stuff we own. But for me, success has become about freedom to do the things I want to do every day . . . quality time with my husband, teaching my children through incredible experiences, and doing work I love from the comfort of my bathrobe and back porch. To me, that screams "success!" every day, and I feel beyond blessed to be able to experience it.

Author and co-founder of Beyond Diet, Isabel De Los Rios has been globally recognized as the "go-to-girl" regarding fat-burning nutrition and exercise programs. Upon graduating from Rutgers University with a degree in exercise physiology, she became a Certified Strength and Conditioning Specialist, the most advanced certification given by the National Strength and Conditioning Association. As an exercise specialist, certified nutritionist, and international bestselling author, Isabel continues to educate clients worldwide with her transformative eating programs that have already restored the health of over 800,000 people.

www.beyonddiet.com

The Power of Prayer

By Shanda Sumpter

I can honestly say my rock star moment is the moment I'm living right now.

I am so blessed to have everything I've ever wanted in life—a husband who adores me, a beautiful baby boy who is the joy of my life, and a booming multimillion-dollar business that's expanding into Europe.

Right now, it looks like I'm on top of the world—and I am. But it wasn't always this way.

For many years, my life was a hot mess.

Before I moved to San Diego, I lived in Las Vegas. I remember at one point, I had $500 cash in an envelope tucked away in my closet, and that was all the money I had in the world. My television was on a cardboard box and I had a towel draped over the box to hide it.

Nothing was working in my life.

I was a Canadian citizen going to school at UNLV, which meant I couldn't get a job, so my friends would lend me money so I could pay bills, and then I would work odd jobs to pay them back. But, of course, the next month was always around the corner, and once it rolled around, there would be more bills, my friends would have to lend me money again, and the cycle would start over again.

I was so broke, it hurt.

At one point, I ended up hooked on cocaine and other drugs. I was engaged to a man who cheated on me. I lost three homes and lost my credit. I had to pay cash for many, many years because I wasn't considered a good credit risk.

But, through it all, I still had a relationship with God. I remember going to church and knowing somewhere inside me that somehow, I was still better than my situation. There was a better way to live and that way was open to me; I just didn't know how to put all the pieces together.

Eventually, I got myself financially stable. I was able to buy a condo, and I had a little money leftover that I ended up investing in real estate.

But then the 2008 real estate crash happened, and again, I lost everything. I had worked so hard to stabilize myself, and just like that, it all came crashing down on me.

It was in this moment that I decided to truly deepen my faith in God. I prayed, and the message I heard was to go to Arizona to work with a shaman. I did, and as I drove back I got the message I needed to teach financial freedom.

What? But I'm not a teacher, a speaker, or an author. I had no business teaching financial freedom.

Nevertheless, the voice persisted. And, in that two-hour drive back to Vegas, I argued with that voice. I had a slew of reasons why I couldn't do it.

Yet, by the time I returned to Vegas, I found myself calling my friend Robert, and together we co-created a program called The Art of Receiving, which was really the beginning of HeartCore Business.

And now, 7 years later, it's a multimillion-dollar business.

One of the beliefs that kept me going even during my worst moments was that bad things aren't happening to hurt us but to strengthen our character so we can receive what we really want in our hearts: our biggest dreams and aspirations.

In my case, what was truly in my heart was living in a house on the ocean, having a husband who cherished me, having children, and never having to worry about money again.

And, that's exactly what I have right now.

My faith in God was what allowed me to drag myself through the mud to get to the other side. Even during my deepest, darkest moments, I still could feel God's presence at my side.

And the deeper my faith, the more I was able to let go of the emotional triggers that would push men away, would push business away, and would push money away. The more I did that, the more life started to open up for me. I was able to take leaps in my life and business—leaps with no net. But every time I did that, not only would the net always appear but the better my life would get.

The deeper I went, the more I was able to let go of the grief and pain of what I was losing and put my faith in God.

I also had to learn to trust on a deeper level. For instance, in 2008 when I lost my home, I was able to live in one of my real estate investments mortgage free for 6 months until the bank foreclosed! This is how I was able to build HeartCore Business without worrying about a place to live.

Yes, I did lose my home, but there's an opportunity in everything, and everything happens for a reason—and that reason is to support you to become everything you've dreamed of.

My faith allowed me to be to more open and to dance with life.

So, if you're someone who is reading this and feeling a call deep inside you to go deeper with your faith, I'd like to invite you to start with a few small steps. Read the Bible, understand scripture, join a church, and pray daily. It may seem a little awkward at first and feel like nothing is happening, but I assure you He is listening and you are being heard. Sometimes it just takes a little time and patience.

My life has turned around because I created a deeper relationship with God. I now have the time freedom, love freedom, and money freedom to do what I want when I want. I have the family I always dreamed of and an amazing business. All of that is possible because of my relationship with God.

And the best part? Even if all of that disappeared tomorrow, I would still have the belief that I could re-create it all because of my relationship with God.

Shanda Sumpter is the founder and Business Lifestyle Expert of HeartCore Business. If you have ever dreamed of having a life of no worries—being able to pay your bills, buying a nice home, sending your kids to college, taking a great vacation, or having the freedom and money to make a difference for others . . . Shanda is the business coach to show you how (and how it may be less complicated than you think).

Shanda is passionate about helping you live your life on your own terms, with her step-by-step system to get your business launched and make money!

www.heartcorebusiness.com/blog

Breaking Up Is Hard to Do
How I Finally Quit Smoking

By Karen Strauss

I was 17—my friend Karen says, "I have something really fun to share with you."

We go down to the bleachers on the football field and she pulls out a pack of Marlboros.

Ooh—something adult—My mother smokes Kents and I always wondered what it was like.

Now was my chance . . . She lights up a cigarette and takes a puff. Obviously, she's been doing this awhile. Me . . . I take a puff and start coughing my brains out.

I felt sick to my stomach—and dizzy . . . but smoking was cool—right?

So, from that day forward—I began to smoke—I stole cigarettes out of my mother's purse.

I got more practiced, stopped coughing, and getting dizzy. Now it was just a nice high feeling.

Plus—if I was smoking then I wasn't eating. My mother used to mention she smoked because she thought she would lose weight because it made her less hungry.

I totally bought into that even though it was obviously not true.

I had no idea at the time that smoking is about the most addicting thing that can happen to you.

It hijacks the brain dopamine pathways the same as illegal drugs. Nicotine dependency is as hard or harder than quitting heroin.

Smoking as a teen can stunt your lungs and lessen your stamina.

I continued to smoke throughout my college years—smoking and drinking were the norms. It was how we relaxed from a hard day of classes, and using our brain to study.

No one talked about the health warnings and how smoking literally kills.

Most of my friends were smokers and my boyfriends either smoked or never seemed to notice that my clothes and breath were tainted . . . I certainly didn't notice.

The first time I tried to quit I was in my late 20's. I had worked hard losing 25 pounds that year—I was in my prime . . . Building my career in publishing, finally at the right weight, and lots of interest from men. The last hurdle was smoking. More facts were made public around then about how harmful smoking was for your health.

So, this was just another challenge I was willing to take on. The one man I was interested in hated smokers. He didn't want them around him, so I refrained from smoking when I was around him.

Major incentive!

I quit cold turkey. That lasted throughout the summer and a little beyond. But within months I started bumming cigarettes from friends. I was gaining a lot of weight back because I was eating instead of smoking. It starts slow—One cigarette a day, turns into 3 cigarettes a day—turns into 10 and before you know it I was back to smoking a pack a day.

FACT: Approximately 70% of smokers want to quit. About 40% try to quit every year.

Of those who try to quit, about 7% stay off nicotine for more than a year. The vast majority do not make it even a week without cigarettes.

I continued to smoke throughout most of my 30's—I curtailed my smoking to about 10 cigarettes a day—convincing myself that I wasn't harming myself since I wasn't smoking a lot.

It really is just as bad a being a drug addict. Hell—I WAS one!

And just like an alcoholic—I was in complete denial.

Once again, I tried to quit. I tried the nicotine gum (disgusting!) and then the patch–and this time it lasted 2 years. I don't really know why after so long I took it up again. I was over the physical effects of the addiction but clearly I wasn't emotionally able to let go.

I don't think I had fully dealt with my mother's death, and I had a breakup with the man who was the love of my life. It was a tragic blow to me and it took me a long time to get over it.

The problem is when you try to quit smoking you might experience these symptoms:

- Urge to smoke
- Depressed mood
- Trouble sleeping
- Irritability
- Frustration
- Anger
- Anxiety
- Difficulty concentrating
- Restlessness
- Decreased heart rate
- Increased appetite or weight gain

I had all of these over the many years and many times I tried to quit.

FINALLY after a few years—I had a breakthrough. One of my closest friends who had been a two pack a day smoker decided to quit. The last person I ever expected to get over his addiction accomplished this amazing feat. I so admired his determination.

A year later, I was at the wedding of one of my employees. A few us would periodically go outside to smoke. It was raining but we persevered.

By the time, I was ready to go home—there was a torrential downpour. My friend and I managed to find a cab—We wound up in a bar next to my house—We had a couple of drinks—went outside to smoke and something inside me snapped! Here I was getting soaked and trying to inhale this wet cigarette—and a voice inside me said—WHAT ARE YOU DOING? You don't even like this. You are putting so much pressure on your lungs that it hurts . . . Why are you doing this do yourself?—You are better than that! AND I suddenly *knew*.

THIS WAS GOING TO BE MY LAST CIGARETTE.

I put it out. Ran home. That was literally the last cigarette I ever smoked in my life . . . 20 years ago.

It was one of the hardest things I ever had to do in life—But I am proud I was able to overcome this nasty addiction

I leave you with this: Don't be one of these statistics:

FACT: Tobacco use causes more than five million deaths a year. For every one person who dies from smoking, twenty more suffer a smoking related illness.

Karen Strauss has worked in publishing for over 30 years holding management and marketing positions at major publishing houses, including Random House, The Free Press, and Crown.

She founded Strauss Consultants in 1991 to work with independent publishers and authors. Karen later founded Hybrid Global Publishing, supplying publishing and marketing services for brands, organizations, and individual authors.

She is the author of Book Publishing For Entrepreneurs: Top Secrets from a New York Publisher.

www.hybridglobalpublishing.com

Love Is the Answer.
It's Always the Answer

By Maryann Ehmann

Have you ever been tooling along smartly in life, when all that you have worked so hard for has come to fruition? Things are great, and you know there's more good in store. Life is pretty darn good. You feel like you're doing things right.

Until something happens. Then something else. And then it's like you get pummeled with lemons, and there doesn't seem to be any time or energy to make the proverbial lemonade. The thing is, it wasn't I that was getting pummeled. It was my husband. But if you are married, and you love your spouse, what happens to them, happens to you.

We had just moved across country from our mini-estate in freezing upstate NY to the warmth and beauty of Scottsdale, AZ. Except for an incessantly crying cat and harrowing, slippery mountain passes, the move was pleasant and exciting. Because of my lovely lifestyle business that I could do from anywhere, the move was barely an interruption. My husband would reestablish his investigative business in our new location. Our savings and the income I generated was plenty to sustain us while he did so. Rather than fly to CA every other month where most of my speaking engagements and networking opportunities were, I could drive and form new relationships locally. At least that was the plan.

Once we were all nicely settled in, the first thing to attend to was finding a surgeon to excise a melanoma on my husband's nose. This would be his 7th procedure, and while inconvenient, he had always recovered excellently. We expected the same again, though we did not realize the stress that would be added from months of downsizing, moving, and finding new doctors. The fact that I was responsible for earning the income and caring for my husband was not something I planned on. Nevertheless, it all worked out fine, and life was good.

Then he was stung by a scorpion. Twice actually, followed by a couple of strange skin rashes and infections. We handled those, as we do, with faith and care, but I was beginning to wonder if something bigger was in play here. Yes, he was evidencing some unusual confusion and uncharacteristic insecurity about finding new clients, but nothing major.

I carried on. I had just come back from CA after spending a productive two days with my client, when my husband started complaining of mild back pain, eventually becoming so severe he could barely breathe.

I rushed him to the hospital where it was determined he had two pulmonary emboli. This was a man who was as strong as an ox, never having even a cold in 14 years. After almost a week in the hospital, he was released with blood thinners in hand. It would be a little while before he could fully recover. Thank God I worked from home.

It was now August, and I was getting a little tired and very distracted. What was happening to my strong, healthy husband? He still wasn't 100%. Nevertheless, being the warrior woman I am, I took my best Sheena stance, stuffing the little voice that said, "I can't do this . . ."

I resumed my work with my clients, more motivated than ever to leverage myself by creating some online courses. But one morning, a few weeks later, Gene informed me that he couldn't read.

"What do you mean you can't read?" I was incredulous. After giving him a passage to test him, it was clear something was wrong, and in a flash I drove him to the ER.

After an MRI and other tests, a nervous doctor entered our room, sputtering, "Um, well, um . . . something is there that doesn't belong there."

What kind of diagnosis it that?!

What he couldn't say that others would was that it was a brain tumor caused by metastasized melanoma. The pulmonary emboli made sense. The confusion of late made sense. Not getting out into the community to find new clients, even that made sense now.

No one knows how long that thing had been growing in my husband's brain, but God, through the hands of well abled doctors—removed it so fast and easily, even they were astounded. In fact, the surgeon said, it just popped out as soon as they opened his head!

A typical 3–5 hour surgery only took 49 minutes, and within an hour after, Gene was alert and pain-free. Within 2 hours, his vision was restored. By all accounts this was miraculous. Within 5 days my husband was sent home, and except for a little fatigue, he was feeling fabulous. In fact, better than he had in a long time. I was ecstatic.

Now, flying high in the grace and goodness of God, you would think I would breathe a sigh of relief and go back to enjoying life and my business. But I couldn't. Something snapped. Instead of peace, heart gripping anxiety took hold of me. Instead of gratitude, I felt alone and without help. I cursed God, accusing Him of abandoning me. It was my job to handle everything, but I needed a little help, and where was He?

My chest felt like it was caving in from hours of uncontrollable crying. Going to bed that night, confused, angry, and feeling very guilty for feeling so, I was inconsolable. What was my problem?! Hadn't we just had a miracle?

The 4 Am Wakeup Call.

At 4 am, I heard the voice of God calling me. "Get back to love, Maryann. Get back to love."

Like in a trance, I quietly stepped out the bedroom, and took out my journal writing, "Dear Lord, I don't know what the heck you are talking about. What does this even mean?"

I realized that my fear, stuffed resentment, and guilty feeling had buried any sensation of love, and I had no idea how to get it back. But almost like my hand had a brain of its own, I began to write pages and pages of miracles and time when God had provided in profound and simple ways. As I wrote, the fear lifted, and my heart began to expand.

In all that was happening all year, my number one fear was not my husband's health. I had uncanny peace and faith about that. Instead it was money. Could I continue to generate income while caring for him? I thought not. Could I be creative with so many distractions? Not a chance. Little voices of fear and doubt had accumulated to cataclysmic proportions.

I am a mindset coach. I help people achieve their dreams. I clear the path so they don't get stuck in negative energy. But I didn't do it for me. I didn't give myself permission to feel the fear, to acknowledge it, and then surrender it to God. Somewhere along the line I started doubting God and His ever present help in time of need.

Nevertheless, God didn't zap me for swearing at Him, doubting Him, or tuning Him out. Instead, He embraced me with Love, sent many faithful prayer partners, and . . . without our asking, provoked the hearts of hundreds of people to get together and gift us with amazing financial gifts.

I learned a huge lesson last year. Love is the answer. Love for yourself. Love for God. Love for others. Love for your purpose, the reason for your being. As I move forward, I am purposing with new resolve to replenish myself daily in Love before I do anything.

After that miraculous surgery and my meltdown, my husband had an extensive hemorrhage in his brain . . . another surgery. But covered in grace, he breezed through that one, too! Now he is finishing his treatments to eradicate the cancer. He is weak but hanging in there.

I don't know what the future holds, but I do know this. I'm not doing this alone. I can't and don't want to. I know who my God is, and He is with us. Selah.

Maryann Ehmann is a speaker, author, income strategist, and mindset master who helps emerging world changers fulfill their dreams and passions, The Magnificent Way™. A former prosecuting attorney, financial adviser, homeschooling mom, and Christian counselor, Maryann believes anyone can create a lifestyle business of their dreams, if they have a strong enough WHY. Maryann is wildly in love with her husband, Gene, and immensely blessed with 4 married children, 11 grandchildren, and 2 great grandkids.

www.MaryannEhmann.com

Expecting Blessings & Miracles

By Janie Lidey

All my life people have asked me, "Janie, why are you so lucky?" After years of contemplating the answer to that question, I came to realize that it has nothing to do with luck and everything to do with how I choose to live my life. I expect blessings & miracles every single day!

In my new book and companion CD, *Leap of Faith ~ 8 Daily Habits To Power Up Your Leap*, I share the habits that have not only made me *seem* lucky but have also made me *feel* like the luckiest girl in the world. I'd like to share a few of those habits with you, give you some samples of what can happen when you expect blessings and miracles, and hopefully light a fire within you that encourages you to implement these habits into your own life making *you* feel like the luckiest girl/guy in the world.

The three habits I have chosen to share with you are *Begin It Now*, *Leap with Love,* and *Act as If.*

Begin It Now

After teaching music in Alaska for twenty-six years, I stepped out of the safety and comfort of one classroom to make the entire world my classroom. I had been sharing my daily habits with my students for years and after seeing how they lifted and inspired them, I wanted to share them with the whole universe. The problem with beginning something new is that fear typically sets in and makes it scary to take a leap of faith. Von Goethe said, "Whatever you can do or dream you can, begin it. Boldness has genius, power and magic in it. Begin it now." What I have learned on my journey is that when you begin something, whether with tiny steps or giant leaps, a myriad of blessings come your way. When I began taking steps toward my dream, surprise money showed up, opportunities appeared, and blessings and miracles began to happen. I took a leap of faith, grew my wings on the way down, and ended up flying high. As John Burroughs said, "Leap and the net will appear."

Leap with Love

Now more than ever, it's so important to choose love over fear. Both are contagious! We all have the power within to be love, share love, and spread the ease of love. The Dalai Lama said, "The more we truly desire to benefit others, the greater the strength and confidence we develop and the greater the peace and happiness we experience. Through love, through kindness, through compassion we establish understanding between ourselves, and others." Since retiring early, I continue to 'wake up' to why I am here and how I can serve. The more I lean into my gift from a place of love, the more I am making a difference in people's lives.

Act as If

We have the power to start creating our day before we even let our feet hit the floor. We can choose to *Act as If* blessings and miracles already exist for us and because we believe we will see them, we do. I'd like to share one of my *Act as If* stories with you.

On January 12, 2016, I received an email from my mentor inviting me into his elite $25,000 per year Mastermind Program. He invited a small number of people to join and was only looking for eight members to fill the group. Once full, the group would be closed. I had to act fast! My mentor's goal was to help turn each of us into Rock Stars in our industry. I wanted to be part of this amazing opportunity. As always, I had woken up that day *Acting as If,* and here was my blessing! The question was, how was this blessing going to become a miracle? Not only did I not have the $25,000, I also had a lot of credit card debt from publishing books, recording CDs, and traveling to events all over the country to become the best I could be in my desire to serve. Part of *Acting as If* is saying yes and figuring it out as you go. So I said yes to the blessing, and the miracle appeared. The same week that I got this invitation, my sister Sue, who had been cleaning homes for a living nearly all of her life, received a large sum of money from one of her longtime clients who had recently passed away. She left half of her estate to my sister, and what turned my blessing into a miracle was that my sister Sue told me she felt like God had given her this money so that she could help me 'make it big' because I had been telling her for years that I wanted to 'make it big' so I could help her!

I believe we are all meant to serve in our own unique and special way. Sometimes it takes a big chunk of our lifetime to realize what our purpose is and then it can be scary to figure out how to lean into our gift. What I do know from my own experience is that, rather than going through life with the mindset of needing to see it to believe it, what we really need to do is believe it and we will see it. I believed that I could be an Amazon #1 Best Selling Author and now I am. I believed that I could record my songs in Nashville with some of the best musicians on the planet and now I have. I also believed that becoming a professional speaker and sharing my music and message around the country would be the perfect way to lean into my gift and share it with others. Now I am now doing exactly that!

I wish you all Blessings & Miracles on your journey.

Janie Lidey is an Emmy award winning songwriter, professional speaker, Amazon #1 best-selling author, and recording artist. Janie speaks and sings at women's conferences, personal growth seminars, music festivals, and more encouraging her audience members to lean into their gift, lose their fear, take a leap of faith, and live the life of their dreams.

www.janielidey.com

"Finnley," an Inspirational Story of Love, Hope, and Faith

By Stephanie Adriana Westover

Finnley, our Shetland sheep dog and my daughter Shana have always had such a great relationship. My husband Val and I decided that it was time that Shana and Finnley should be together. For an Easter present, we drove to Shana's house and gave Finnley to her.

May 19th—Finnley was home alone with Shana's house cleaner. Leaving a door open, the house cleaner didn't realize that Finnley went outside. About an hour had passed before she noticed that Finnley was nowhere to be found. Shana called me later in a completely panic. Val and I dropped everything that we were doing and raced to join Shana to search for Finnley. You could hear all of us yelling and whistling for Finnley all night long. We searched everywhere until 2 a.m. with no success. It was as if he had just vanished. This was so devastating, as Finnley is such a huge part of our family.

May 20th—The next day, Shana began putting missing dog posters on every post that she could find. Val and I contacted every dog pound and shelter possible. Since Finnley was properly registered with tags, name, and phone number on his collar, if found, he would be tracked back to us. Later that day, Shana received two phone calls. One from someone who saw Finnley at a fitness center and one who saw him at a local park. Once again, we concentrated our search in these two areas with no success. With

Shana's neighborhood bordering a vast wilderness area, we had deep concerns for his safety from coyotes, rattle snakes, mountain lions, and lack of food. Another concern was that if someone saw him, they would have a hard time catching him because he is frightened of strangers. Every day, we all would search the areas were Finnley was last seen.

May 23rd—Four days after Finnley's disappearance. Shana called us and she said that a family just saw Finnley running up a hill in a wilderness area. We were on scene within 15 minutes of her call. Shana was already there and said that she saw Finnley run up over a cactus and brush covered hill. With our Border Collie "Monty" by Val's side, he scoured the hills for miles, while Shana and I combed through the surrounding neighborhoods. Once again, no trace of Finnley. Later that evening after treating Val for poison oak, I put the word out on all of my social media channels to be on the lookout for Finnley. Many good friends put the word out to their network of friends. We had so much positive support and encouragement from so many wonderful people. We also heard amazing personal survival stories from others which gave us hope.

May 24th—Val and I received an upsetting phone call from Shana. She told us that someone had called her and told her that they just witnessed Finnley being hit by a car. They said that she could find his body on the roadside by a local school. We all raced to that location expecting to see our beloved dog dead on the side of the road. We couldn't find Finnley anywhere. We later found out that the call Shana received was a cruel hoax. Every day after that was spent again putting up flyers, talking to people and searching neighborhoods and wilderness areas.

June 7th—Nineteen days after Finley's disappearance. Val and I were searching a part of the wilderness that was in proximity to were Finnley was spotted in the past when we came across some fresh bones. The more we searched, the more bones we found. We pieced them together and they resembled our Finnley. We put the bones in a bag and brought them home. We decided that if there was no further trace of Finnley after a month had passed by, the bones are most likely his and we need to bury him and say our goodbyes. Not wanting to accept the fact that we could have found Finnley's bones, we all continued our daily routine in searching.

June 21st—Father's Day. Thirty-three days after Finnley's disappearance. Even though it has been over a month since his disappearance, we still hadn't buried our Finnley's bones. Val and I were just about ready to sit down for our Father's Day dinner with our parents when Val's cell phone rang. A girl's voice on the other end of the phone said, "Hi, my name is Mel and I have your dog Finnley, I think he got out and I was able to catch him!" Not wanting to get everyone's hopes up, Val asked me to keep our parents entertained while he raced out of the house and headed towards the address that Mel gave him. Mel was waiting in front of her home with our Finnley! Val could not believe his eyes. Mel told Val that Finnley went into her backyard and was crying for food. She was able to lure Finnley to her with food and that is how she was able to catch him. Val couldn't thank her enough as he explained to her that Finnley had been missing since May 19th. Val spent the next ten minutes loving and squeezing a very excited Finnley. There wasn't a dry eye to be found.

Val called me and told me that he had Finnley in the car. I started crying and asked if he was alive. He told me that other than being skin and bones, he looked incredible. I then called my daughter Shana to tell her the news, she could not stop crying and said that she would be right over.

This experience has helped me to know that when I'm faced with life's challenges, that I should never give up believing in love, hope, and faith.

Award-winning Celebrity Photographer Stephanie Adriana Westover specializes in Portraits, Weddings and Fine Art Photography. Stephanie's work can be found in Galleries, Hotels, Restaurants, Homes and Businesses around the world.

Since 2010 Stephanie and her husband Val Westover have traveled to 20 major cities in the US, Europe and Canada teaching "The

Basic Elements of Photography" to over *25,000 participants. Stephanie enjoys her "Epic Life" with Val, seven beautiful children and menagerie of incredible animals.*

www.ValWestoverPhotography.com

Determined to Slay the Dragon

By Lesley Nardini

Growing up, I didn't have a lot of confidence or belief in myself. My parents divorced when I was just 4 years old and, being the 4th out of 5 kids, I felt like I got lost in the shuffle. As a result I often felt neglected and left to my own devices. My sister and I lived with our mom and my brothers went to live with our dad. I desperately missed having a male influence in my life. We moved around a lot and, being the new kid, I often got picked on. When I was in grade school, I frequently got into fist fights with other kids. I was tough, angry and often unhappy as a young girl. The one good thing that came out of this is that I learned to be self-sufficient and resilient. I had to fend for myself a lot and this instilled a sense of determination in me which has served me well in life.

While I was determined and self-sufficient I also lacked self-confidence, self-esteem and belief in myself. Adding to my low self-worth, I had a string of "failures" in Jr. High and High School. I tried out for absolutely everything that came my way (cheerleading, dance team, student government, drill team, flag carrier, talent shows, basketball team, you name it) and was never picked for anything. I felt like a loser and carried myself like a loser. I struggled with my weight and remember getting teased about this which had an impact on my body image. I was often unhappy but my determination kept me going. In my senior year I decided to try out to be a contestant in the Miss Tustin scholarship pageant. Thirty girls tried out for 20 spots so I felt my odds were pretty good. Once again, my name was not called. I was devastated! I felt so low and rejected I wanted to give up on trying out for anything ever again. This is where my dad's influence came into the picture.

By this time I had made the choice to live with my dad and stepmother which provided much needed stability and support in my life. My dad taught me the power of a positive attitude and he was very encouraging to me after this crushing failure. What happened next was a pivotal moment in my life. A few days after I was rejected I got a call from the committee saying that one of the girls had dropped out and I was the first alternate. Finally, I had been picked for something. It didn't matter that I made the cut as an alternate. It didn't matter that I didn't win the pageant or place as a semi-finalist. Still, I felt like a winner. It was one of the happiest moments of my life. The experience changed me in so many ways and it gave me a huge boost of confidence that has stayed with me for life.

Because of this positive experience I got hooked on pageants. It's one of the places where I experienced success and I wanted more of that feeling. I proceeded to compete in multiple pageants over the next several years. Once again, I had a string of failures while competing that gnawed away at my confidence. My view of myself as a "loser" didn't go away easily. Fear and doubt always crept in to get the better of me, making me nervous and affecting my confidence. When my dad died unexpectedly around my 22nd birthday it was a devastating blow that set me back. I spent a few years after his death in a dark place and I made a lot of bad decisions. However, my determination kept me going. I kept working on myself to become a better, stronger, more confident person. I read books and attended seminars to learn what it takes to be successful. I started noticing a pattern in these books and seminars and realized that if I simply followed the "recipe for success" my life would improve. Slowly but surely my confidence and belief in myself grew. Small successes lead to bigger successes. One of my greatest achievements happened 20 years after my first pageant when I was crowned as Mrs. Oregon. This was meaningful to me in ways that I can't even describe. It felt like a lifetime of fear, self-doubt, and low self-esteem had been slain like a giant dragon.

I discovered something else that was a big surprise to me. I thought that when I won that pageant and slayed that giant dragon, my fear and self-doubt would magically disappear forever. I was shocked to find it's always lurking somewhere behind me, trying to invade my thoughts and hold me back from having the life of my dreams. It's a sneaky, persistent monster that is ready to pounce if I ever let down my guard.

I've learned that the best way to keep it at bay is to consistently strengthen my heart, mind and soul by reading books, attending motivational seminars and networking with success-minded people. This is one principle that is common in every book and seminar on achievement and success. Regular exercise for the body, mind and spirit gives us the strength, resilience and confidence to slay any dragon that comes our way.

Another important lesson I've learned is that the basic rules I applied to win that pageant also apply to being successful at absolutely anything in life. I applied these same principles to my marriage and parenting. My husband and I have been married for 35 years and both of our children are amazing, successful adults. I applied these principles to job searching in mid-life and was able to land 3 incredible jobs in my fifties. I'm now applying these success principles to my journey of fulfilling my lifelong dream to be a successful speaker and author. I'm well on my way to achieving this goal! Nothing great happens by accident.

After years of struggling to find her confidence and feminine power, Lesley Nardini found the "Recipe for Success". She is now living her lifelong dream of being a speaker, author, and success coach, helping other women find their passion, power, and purpose to live their best life.

www.LesleyNardini.com

Climbing over Rocks

By Naomi Carmona-Morshead

I am committed to climbing over boulders; overcoming obstacles. I've reached the top many times: marriage, children, entrepreneur, business owner, awards, achievements, grandchildren, prayer warrior and more. I've also experienced many valleys: car accidents, death of spouse, financial loss, and miscommunication. I've learned it's when you have mountain-top life experiences, your perspective changes. The higher you climb; the better the view! Thank you God for mountain top experiences!

I climb mountains. In 2015, I climbed 8 mountains in 8 months. But it wasn't always that way. I was born in 1954 with a congenital heart defect. Even with surgical intervention, my chances were only 50/50. I survived pioneering open heart surgery 50 years ago at age 10. But I wasn't strong. I didn't know I had the potential for physical activity. I chose to conquer mental, physical, emotional, and spiritual obstacles starting at age 58. I decided to make a "Brave Heart Shift" and was trained with doctor's advice using resources & focus to become stronger than ever!

I climbed the tallest free-standing mountain in the world—Mt. Kilimanjaro, Tanzania, Africa, 19,341 feet elevation last year. At 13,000 feet, before we reached the summit, I woke up at 2 am. I fumbled for my jacket, my knit cap, head lamp and unzipped the first door of the tent, and then the outer door. As I made my way out, I had to close each zipper in freezing temperature. I stood up in a pitch black night. Above me were four trillion stars. My eyes adjusted and I discovered right in front of me that I was standing equal to the Big Dipper. Really! I had climbed the mountain *to the stars* to save "little hearts" for Mending Kids. I had reached my goal!

> Today, you are exactly where you are supposed to be. There is someone who needs your service, your hug, your smile, your love, your "Big Dipper," your "Brave Heart Shift."

Next we climbed to 16,000 feet elevation. It was seven difficult hours climbing UP, UP, UP to hike 2.3 miles. Why? One step forward; slide back; one step forward; slide back; one step forward; slide back. *In the game called LIFE, You are a virtual mountain climber and you need to know HOW to climb the mountain of life, don't you? One step at a time.* We stopped after a rock scramble at 18,652 feet, Gilman's Point. To recover and rest, they served us hot tea and biscuits. *Daily life needs rest!*

We hiked to Stella Point, 18,885 feet. The air is quite thin. In fact, it's harder to breathe; you <u>must</u> walk slowly. "Naomi, you lead; follow the path down into the crater."

I couldn't see more than three feet ahead. As I walked down into the fog, there were rocks as big as a VW car. Walking slowly through the fog; the air was freezing; it began to snow.

"Don't you want to lead the group?" I said.

M'hina, the guide answered "Keep walking."

I walked slowly for one and a half hours. Suddenly there was a big darkness with a man standing just in front of me. It was our mess tent with hot food, refreshments, and rest!

> Who supports you as you climb the mountain of life? Do you ask them for help? Do they say "Keep walking!"? You are a virtual mountain climber: you climb UP and you help others reach the summit and then rest.

In 2009, I met a little Ecuadoran girl (9), Maria Jose, visiting the USA for open heart surgery and scoliosis. Her procedures were provided by Mending Kids, Burbank, CA.

In the ICU watching Maria, I re-experienced my ICU days (50 years prior) when I was 10 years old lying in an oxygen tent with tubes everywhere.

Seeing little Maria survive two surgeries inspired me to dedicate the rest of my life to raising money to provide heart surgeries for underserved children around the world.

Today I am a healthy 62-year-old. From a non-athlete, my husband trained me to summit real mountains and virtual mountains of life.

Why was it important to get to the summit? I received a vision; I understood that God had a message for me that I could learn at that top of Mt. Kilimanjaro.

M'hina started talking, "Naomi, you prayed for snow and it snowed. Because of the snow, it's too foggy. There won't be any sun today until we hike down in a few hours."

"But there's going to be sun, I just know it!" I said.

The first 200 yards it was foggy, a bit of pink in the sky. As we reached the summit sign, yellow light burst through the fog; it was brilliant sun! It lasted for 20 minutes. There <u>was</u> something to experience at the summit. M'hina was right. I could not see the ground for a cloud covered the entire summit of the mountain. But I got the message.

<u>"Leave the darkness behind and walk into the light."</u>

> Is that message for you? What darkness is holding you
> back? What obstacle is keeping you in the dark? Darkness
> will speak, "There's not going to be any sun." You don't
> have to listen. Leave the darkness behind. You CAN climb
> up no matter how many steps you take backwards. You will
> reach the summit of your life.

I call this process "The Brave Heart Shift." <u>YOU</u> make the decision to Shift towards the light. Combine resources and training and focus both towards a goal. You will gain courage and compassion which become heart-centered: SHIFT!

Your goal may be big or small incremental steps. I challenge you to turn towards the light and make a Brave Heart Shift in your life today.

Naomi Carmona-Morshead speaks internationally, climbs mountains, and escorts tours. She is a wife/widow, mother/grandmother, entrepreneur, and health architect. She tells tales about hiking trails so difficult, she could only take 100 steps before resting. She has overcome physical, mental, and emotional obstacles to reach the summit of Mt. Kilimanjaro in Africa.

Mending 100 Hearts fundraising has already saved nineteen children.

If you'd like to help me, donate here: www.Mendingkids.Org. REF: 100 Hearts.

Follow my adventure blog: www.Mending100Hearts.wordpress.com

www.TheBraveHeartShift.com

The Gift of Cushing's

By Robin deGroot

I have many things to be grateful for in my life but I never expected having Cushing's disease would be one. I am not quite sure of the cause since I had many health problems when I was young. My early years were rocky. I screamed the nights away the first year if my mother laid me down, since the pressure in my ears did not change, as it should when horizontal so my mother slept with me in an upright position most often. When I was nearly one year old, I had a life-threatening fall down the stairs in a walker. I survived but gave my mother a terrible scare. The MMR vaccination landed me in the hospital with dangerously high fever twice and it has never successfully incited anti-bodies. I experienced many intense food sensitivities that created an excess of mucous and skin issues. I had chronic earaches until I was five. Around that age, I had my tonsils removed and tubes placed in my ears. I became free of my constant congestion after these procedures, along with the avoidance cow's milk and products.

Life was better after that for a few years. When I was around seven years old, my mother began working for a chiropractor and naturopath. She was always interested in holistic health but now she took her qualifications as a Registered Nurse into the holistic health field. She was very happy to find supportive information regarding food as healing that she had suspected for a long time. I started developing female hormonal attributes when I was eight years old, so our Naturopathic doctor looked into my health further. He discovered that I had nerve rings in my eyes, signi-fying issues with my central nervous system. Stress needed to be managed; foods with hormones should be avoided, and I should jump on the rebounder daily to stimulate my compromised lymphatic system.

I was already used to diet restrictions so this was not extremely difficult, just not fun. Perhaps this contributed to my seriousness at this age. The days of drawing and playing 'Cindys' with my sister seemed so far away by then. With the hormonal development came weight gain and I was not happy with either of those. At that age, I could join the synchronized swimming team at last and that was a milestone I was waiting for. I joined my mother and three older sisters on the team. Soon after I also joined the competitive swim team, and finally at nine years old my weight and early hormone development subsided. I admired the beautiful, graceful bodies of my older sisters and aspired to the same. Eventually, however, the same problems of before always-threatened return without intense steady exercise and a keen eye on the foods I ate.

On family trips the diet restrictions were difficult. The family seemed to be split into two groups and I was jealous of those who could eat whatever they liked without problems. I still held onto faith that my good habits would yield the perfection I sought in the long run. In middle school, I struggled with all of the same things, plus added social awkwardness after moving away from my old school. Playing soccer outside with friends was no longer the norm and I seemed to be alone now. In high school I set out to create changes. I cut my hair very short one year to grow it all one length, and started cross-country to make big changes. I began running seriously in high school. By then I participated in sailing, tennis, karate, figure skating, gymnastics, and of course—swimming for many, many years. I took piano lessons for one year but found little time to practice. I am still set on learning music. I did not realize it then but my condition contributed to my success. Though athletics kept my weight in check and fueled my inner drive and competitive side, I felt little pain while over training. I was an overachieving perfectionist; ultimately quite successful at most things I tried.

I graduated high school and went to university when I was sixteen, graduating from university when I was nineteen. In university, I noticed hair growing on my neck and chin, slightly at first but then soon much more. I did not know yet that an excessive amount of the hormone cortisol was helping me with my physical abilities and handling unbelievable stress, but also creating side effects of low thyroid like symptoms, weight gain, and facial hair. I worked with my art teachers to let go of perfectionism through the healing medium of art and worked on more spiritual and passionate messages instead. When practicing life drawings, I saw beauty in the naked human form. I modeled nude on occasion to conquer my own self-consciousness, perfectionism, and criticism of my body.

When I went out to dance clubs, I felt beautiful, free, creative, and true to my soul. I met my husband at a gothic alternative dance club in Montreal. The summer after graduation I discovered I was pregnant. I was excited and anxious and ready to move in a new direction. Our daughter was born in the spring of 1996 and she became my 'everything.' I did not know the searing stretch marks I received from this pregnancy were not normal until after I had lost all the baby weight through nursing. They were purple tears and I was also developing a large fatty pad between my shoulders. I went to a somatic body-worker in Vancouver on my family's recommendation and she noticed that the symptoms seemed to indicate Cushing's disease. Finally, I had a clue for lifelong anomalies.

I had moved to California by then, partly to be in a progressive area of the world for health and to research this condition. From 1999 to 2014, I was tested and monitored, as I lived out the next phase of my life. My son was born; I learned about QiGong energy practice; my mother passed away; I was a Montessori teacher for seven years until leaving the field over stress; I ran a business as a massage therapist and Energetic chakra body worker; and became an entrepreneur. Finally, after fourteen years of testing, I was approved for surgery to remove the tumor from my pituitary gland. This small tumor sent incorrect hormonal messages to my adrenals, which in turn created an overproduction of the hormone cortisol (a more misunderstood important adrenal hormone), causing facial hair growth, stretch marks, weight gain, a back hump, round face, high blood sugar, high blood pressure, and years of constant anxiety; but also energy, and decreased inflammation.

I lost forty pounds after surgery and my face became defined for the first time. I still practice a healthy diet for optimum weight, calm, and clarity. I still have high personal drive, but do experience more pain and less tolerance for high levels of stress now. My goals now are to help others heal. I learned that the pituitary gland represents control, as it controls the glandular system. This mirrors my lifetime effort to find my voice of personal empowerment within relationships and amongst my large family. I have personally experienced inner stress manifest into physical ailments. My life's work now focuses on helping people remove emotional trauma energetically. I have gained intense appreciation for outer problems exposing inner pain and learned that hormones have an immense effect on our health, looks, longevity, sleep, strength, will, drive, and emotions. I am grateful for all that Cushing's disease taught me.

Robin deGroot is a coach, trainer, writer, and speaker, facilitating soul expression through her TLC (Truth•Love•Creativity) system. Robin's talents with art, chakra healing, writing and divining, enrich her podcast, online presence, and live programs. Robin lives in the San Francisco bay area, along with her husband and two children.

www.RobinMdeGroot.com

Not Necessarily Where I Ought to Be

By Melanie Fatuesi

Becoming a Woman Who Rocks was a process that took years. Standing in that truth is a strength I found after a happenstance meeting with Dr. Bill Mitchell of Dale Carnegie Training.

In 2009, I was in the US after spending years overseas. My son, Luka, was a member of the Chapin Marching Band out of El Paso, Texas, where I still reside. Always happy to help out where I can, I'd volunteered as a bus monitor and set about recruiting other parents to help chaperon the band's football games. I didn't give a thought to who might be watching, just got organized, set an example, and grabbed opportunities to inspire others. After a couple months building a well-organized team, a dad of one of the band kids pulled me aside.

He knew I'd been looking for a job. When he asked if I wanted to work for him, I said, "Of course!" He was surprised that I hadn't asked what the job entailed, but as I explained to him, as long as it didn't require me to do anything illegal or immoral, I was up for any challenge. Bill, the dad in question, hired me on the spot, putting me in charge of scheduling his speaking engagements and other activities of Dale Carnegie Training in El Paso. Applying the personal and professional skills I gained at Dale Carnegie empowered me to embrace a new career as a dynamic leader and educator in the business community.

Though Bill's offer came out of the blue, the skills that caught his attention certainly did not.

Comparing my early life in Swartz Creek, Michigan to where I am today is a study in contrast. My dad was an illiterate factory worker whose economic outlook depended on the stability of US manufacturing. During in my junior year of high school, I had to depend on food stamps and public assistance to survive. Along with my classmates and thousands of underemployed Americans, I was looking towards an uncertain future. I saw the writing on the wall when General Motors initiated a wave of layoffs and was no longer hiring. Not content to accept the economic decline as my personal destiny, I enlisted in the army at the age of eighteen.

For six years, I trained and served alongside the bravest men and women I've ever met. The army catalyzed my drive to be the best I can be. After finishing basic training at Fort McClellan, I served as an MP and in just over two years achieved my goal of making sergeant, becoming one of the few female non-commissioned officers to lead a combat team up to that time. Deployments to Korea, Panama, Honduras, and Guantanamo Bay expanded my worldview. My combat deployment to Somalia taught me the importance of ingenuity and gave me the strength to be rock solid leader.

Motherhood brought new challenges. Having left the military to start a new family, I became determined to help Luka achieve his dreams and the boundless possibilities I saw in his heart and mind. Pursuing that goal, I taught him to read before he could ride a bike, pouring out my time and energy in ways I hadn't known were possible. The guiding light that Dr. Mitchell and the Dale Carnegie Course provided came along at just the right time to help propel Luka through the critical high school years. In just a few short months from the time of writing, I look forward to being the proud mother of a Stanford University graduate.

My journey as a leader has benefited greatly from the mentoring I've received. One milestone along that journey was joining Toastmasters International. After years of inching towards an understanding of how to succeed, achieve, and lead, I made up my mind to qualify as a Distinguished Toastmaster, a distinction held by less than 1% of my fellow members. I completed the exhaustive requirements in just over eighteen months. As part of my curriculum, I founded a speech club at La Tuna Federal Correctional

Institution. It was my privilege to help inmates prepare to rejoin society equipped with new ideals and aspirations.

The life I lead now is nothing like the future I imagined for myself and my peers back when I was eking out an existence on welfare. While many were content to ride the sinking economic tide in a downward spiral, all I wanted was to find a way to escape the cycle of uncertainty and dependency. Thanks to the hardships I've endured, the soldier's ethos I adopted as my own, the leaders who reached out to me and my wonderful family, I've done more than I ever thought possible. My current position as a nurse recruiter for a major corporate hospital provides an outlet for my organizational ambitions. But the work I find most rewarding is inspiring individuals and companies to unleash their hidden potential as a motivational speaker. The seminars and boot camps I host are greenhouses of personal growth. I love the feedback and energy I get from these events. Everyone is an opportunity to shine.

On the road from the Rust Belt to the Sun City, my attitude of achievement has been tested many times. But I've never lost sight of where I started, I've never regretted the race I've run, and I've never forgotten the people who helped me along the way. There's no finish line to this marathon. As long as my family, friends, mentors, and tribe keep encouraging me, I'll never stop succeeding, achieving, and leading.

First Lady Rosalyn Carter said it best, "A leader takes people where they want to go. A great leader takes people where they don't necessarily want to go, but ought to be." My own example shows that if you live with passion and take action even when you think nobody's watching, you can transform yourself and the world around you. Don't confuse where you are with where you ought to be. Step out of your dreams and start living your vision! I'm rooting for you~

Melanie Fatuesi hales from Swartz Creek, Michigan. She joined the Army at 18 and has traveled the world, serving from Somalia to Guantanamo to Korea.

Melanie has won several awards for speaking and has earned her Distinguished Toastmaster.

Melanie has one son, Luka who is currently attending Stanford University and she resides in El Paso TX.

www.succeedachievelead.com

Face-to-Face Time

By Mary Beth Gilbert

"Is it not to share your food with the hungry and to provide the poor wanderer with shelter—when you see the naked, to clothe him, and not to turn away from your own flesh and blood? Then your light will break forth like the dawn, and your healing will quickly appear; then your righteousness will go before you and, and the glory of the LORD will be your rear guard." The Book of Isaiah 58:7–8 (NIV)

"He has shown you, O man, what is good. And what does the LORD require of you? To act justly and to love mercy and to walk humbly with your God." The Book of Micah 6:8 (NIV)

Oh my . . . I would have never thought after learning my mother had been pregnant nine times and gave birth to four beautiful children during her twenties, that I would have any problem getting pregnant myself one day. Just knowing she was pregnant so many times made me think once that when my husband, Daniel, and I got married, we would conceive if we even looked at each other in a loving way.

However, as the years went, on we tried and tried! After many infertility tests, three surgeries, hundreds of prayers, thousands of dollars, people praying over us from all over the world, trying anything I could . . . food, vitamins, etcetera, to help get pregnant, my womb still was not opening. We tried month after month for 17 years!

About five years after we started trying, I had come to my wit's end and called another friend of mine, who was a pastor's wife, hoping to get some consolation as I knew she had struggled with infertility for a certain amount of time as well. Hoping she would console me, listen to all my woes, and have a little pity party with me, but she did just the opposite. After a brief, but sweet conversation, she directed me straight to the Lord to spend more time with Him about it and hung up the phone. I was a bit perplexed!

My husband was in South Korea for a ministry conference and I was all alone. So, I did what my friend suggested, I shut all the blinds in our little graduate school housing apartment, prayed, and worshipped the Lord.

That evening ended up being a very special experience. It was such a close time with the Lord, so close that the Holy Spirit led me to take communion privately in my home. Yes, just between the Lord and me, where I said from the depth of my heart, "Lord, I will worship you whether you give us children or not."

It was one of those life experiences you just have to crawl up in His lap and find rest and peace in Him to see you through.

However, as the Lord always does . . . He brought beauty and joy out of pain and disappointment from 17 years of infertility.

In 1988, my husband and I went to Asia to encourage missionaries. One of the places we visited was South Korea. While there, I grew in love with orphaned children and mentioned to my husband on our way back to the States, "if God ever led us to adopt, I would love to adopt from South Korea."

Little did I know that would actually be in His plan one day. What I thought would happen regarding children was we would have some biological children and then adopt from South Korea. But instead, God never saw fit to give us biological children but He did see fit to give us our hearts desire to adopt a special little girl from South Korea when she was only four months old.

The pain of infertility seemed to just evaporate by the all-encompassing joy this little life brought into our hearts and our home.

When our daughter, Maria, was a baby through toddlerhood, every evening after reading her a story before bedtime, I would sit in a rocking chair and place her on my lap with her head on my knees facing me. We would have a sweet face-to-face time.

One night around Christmas when our daughter was almost 3 years old, she saw pictures of Mary when she was pregnant with baby Jesus. She said to me, "Mommy, I came from your tummy?" I said, "Honey, you came from my heart." Thinking in literal terms, she said, "your heart must have been real big" to which I replied, "it was SO BIG, it was this big," and I stretched both of my arms wide open. Her precious little face looked at me with amazement.

God's heart is SO BIG for you and me that He stretched His arms wide open for us on the cross filled with so much love.

Sometimes when life gives us pain and disappointments, we just need to crawl up in "God's lap" and have some face-to-face time. Time to pray, rest, trust Him, trust His ways, be thankful, cherish good memories, make more good memories, be helpful to others, endure, still smile, because joy will come in the morning and no one loves you greater than your Heavenly Father.

The following are some questions to contemplate for your life:

Do you need to have some face-to-face time with the Lord so He can amaze you with His love, His ideas, His hope?

Is there something you need to take private communion over between you and the Lord?

Why not tell Him you will choose to worship Him whether or not He answers a deep concern of your heart in your way or in your timing?

Why don't you take time to crawl up into His lap and have some face-to-face time with Him?

Mary Beth Gilbert is passionate about encouraging women to fulfill their destiny in the Lord. She is a Bible teacher and international woman's speaker whom God has used to impact thousands of lives around the world. Mary Beth has served in the ministry for over 25 years, even as she has worked in the business and academic worlds. She is married to Dr. Daniel Gilbert, Ph.D. and has a daughter and lives in Southern California. To learn more about Mary Beth's amazing story and to have her speak at your church, Bible Study or conference, you can contact her at: MaryBeth@EmPowered-Living.org

www.EmPowered-Living.org

Listen to the Nice Police Officer

By Bonnie Kitahata

After hearing my side of the story, the nice police officer urged me, "Get back in there and fight!"

About 5 months prior, while I was working full-time at the Los Angeles Police Department as a clerk typist, I got accepted into nursing school. Officer 'Nice' was very encouraging and thought I'd be a great nurse. I decided to keep my job while in the nursing program just in case I didn't end up liking it. But whoa! It was tough! Learning to "help people" is a lot harder and more complicated and challenging that I had imagined!

Well, don't tell anybody, but I flunked out of my second semester of nursing school. Ugh, how embarrassing! As I told my family and friends of my failure, they were all sympathetic and said things like, "Oh, well, you already have a good job." or "Nursing is a terrible job anyway." Except for Officer Nice. As I think back, I believe that his one emphatic sentence changed my life forever. "Get back in there and fight!"

I did get back into the nursing program, this time with more determination and discipline . . . and yay, graduated the nursing program and passed the California State Nursing Boards. So, since 1985, I have been a registered nurse.

Now I could go on and on about how I've saved lives, comforted the sick and downtrodden, given my patients encouragement and hope, resuscitated and rescued the compromised, eased their pain and nausea, reassured the anxious ones, and calmed the crazies, blah blah blah. But I'm not going to do that.

Instead, I want to express my gratitude.

Because of being a nurse, yes, I've been able to 'help people'. But more importantly, I have been privileged to meet people from all walks of life. I've gotten to hear their stories, about themselves, their families, their pets, their hobbies, their struggles and triumphs. I've been inspired by my patients' courage, resolve, and determination. Their jokes and laughter as they recover make my days brighter.

I recently wrote a blog post about some wonderful thank-you gifts that I have received over the years from my patients. But the most wonderful and enduring gifts are gifts to my spirit.

Dorothy was one of my most inspiring gifts. I had not slept well that night, and I came into work a little sluggish and feeling sorry for myself. My legs were achy from the hectic shift the day before. As I walked into Dorothy's room, the first thing I see is her pleasant, smiling face. "Oh, I hate to bother you, because I know you are so busy, but I've been trying to turn myself and I'm just stuck!" She's in her 60's, and has had a progressively debilitating disease for several years. Both of her legs are flaccid, and she has straps around each one so that she can pull the straps to reposition them. She is (was) right-handed but could barely move her right arm then. Her left arm and hand have general motor function, which she uses to reposition her other limbs.

Oh boy, I immediately snapped out of my woe-is-me syndrome and jumped to nurse-to-the-rescue. It was not hard to reposition her, she was a tiny thing; used a lot of pillows to fluff and comfort her . . . so that she felt 'just right'. She had such a positive attitude . . . she was so appreciative of my help, of that little thing I could do for her . . . She chatted cheerily about her grandkids and how she was teaching them how to take care of flowers and plants in the garden like she used to love to do, about how she works on a computer that she can talk into, and how she loved watching old reruns of Seinfeld.

She could barely move and was confined to a bed, and yet she was one of the most positive people I have ever met. It was a really hectic day that day, but I checked on her as much as possible, and each time we shared stories and some laughs, and she actually encouraged me through my day as much as I encouraged her through her treatments and recovery. Shame on me for complaining about my aching legs and lack of sleep! I think of her often, as she has been an inspiration for my career . . . and my life.

It's a good thing that I did listen to that nice police officer. If it wasn't for him I might not have gotten into my rewarding career of nursing and meeting and caring for my patients like Dorothy. Not that all patients are like her. No, of course not. I might go as far as to say that most are not. But the ones who are, are the ones I choose to have the most influence on me. I hope that I impart those positive influences on my patients, and on my co-workers and others around me: Kindness, encouragement and hope.

Bonnie Kitahata has been a nurse since 1985 and has worked in ICU, DOU, radiology, operating room, med-surg, float pool, nursing registry, international volunteer, travel nursing, home health, senior home care, and more. She is a patient advocate, nurse advocate, and creator of Breaking Burnout. She is on a mission to help nurses everywhere avoid nurse burnout.

www.BreakingBurnout.com

A Detour from the Plan

By Linda Kruse

Two roads diverged in a wood and I—I took the one less traveled by, and that has made all the difference.

–Robert Frost

I've always been a planner. I made very deliberate decisions to set my life on a very specific course. University. Career. Filmmaking. Home. Family. But then one day, I started on an unplanned journey down that poetically diverged road which led me to an age-old question: If I knew now what I didn't know then . . . would I have taken that road?

Several years ago, I overheard my brother Victor talking about a trip he was planning with his wife and two kids across a country he didn't know: America. You see, Victor was a decorated and soon-to-be retired US Army officer who spent his life defending a country he had never really lived in. He and I both grew up overseas in a military family—and then he went into the Army. He spent over 20 years of service in every major foreign conflict the US was engaged in during that time. He had been planning this huge road trip to find a home for his family for years, and I only heard about it one month before they were to depart! With little to no planning, I decided to tag along and film it, thinking it would make an interesting documentary: "An American Hero's search for an American Hometown."

Now, it's widely known that The Number ONE Rule in Film-making is: "Pre-Production, Pre-Production, Pre-Production." And being a planner, I would've normally kept that in mind. But given the timing I only had two choices: I either join them on this journey, shooting as we go, or miss it altogether by bogging myself down with planning it.

I had saved up a lot of money toward my plan to buy a home in Los Angeles—and well, that cute little house instead paid for me to film a 2-year long figure-8 trip across America, filming in 37 states, and conducting over 600 interviews.

The idea was that we would seek out one small town in each state that would represent an ideal place to live in America. However, what started as a documentary about a family quickly turned into something more:

> *It's the oldest story known to man, coming home, but with a twist . . .*
>
> *After spending most of his life living outside the United States defending his country, now back from the war, where does a decorated 20-year Army soldier go home to—if he's never really had a hometown?*

But this amazing idea got fraught with so many issues; I hired the wrong people, I spent too much money, I lost jobs, I missed opportunities, missteps, misjudgments. So many times, things got derailed, deterred and I got discouraged, dissuaded, and just plain disappointed: mostly in myself and my lack of planning. It had speed bumps with sign after sign saying this was never going to be anything. That I should stop, that I should quit. But "quit" is a word I know not of.

> *To Quit: to depart, drop out, give up, relinquish, renounce, retire, surrender, withdrawal, desert, evacuate, exit, forsake, hang it up, resign . . .*

I lost friends, I lost money, and I lost years of my life working on this ONE project.

But this was supposed to be a motivational story. So here goes . . .

I don't quit. Ever. I don't give up, I don't drop out, don't relinquish, or renounce. I don't surrender, withdrawal, desert, evacuate, exit, or abandon. And I certainly don't hang it up or resign. I just reorganized.

In life, the things that go wrong are often the very things that lead to other things going right.

–Arianna Huffington

Looking closer, I realized *this* story was way bigger than just one family. *THIS* was a universal story, celebrating *community*. I regrouped and reworked the material. I was relentless. I searched and found the right crew. I saved and I spent more money, eventually crafting it all into Season One of KRUSING AMERICA, a 6-part family travel docu-series that follows Lt. Colonel Victor Krus and his family as they crisscross the country on a quest to find their home, sweet home.

How did I find my way? I went back to the *one* thing that resonated more than the story, the family, or even the trip. The *one* thing that made all the difference was *the kindness of strangers*. In each town, I was reminded over and over of the unexpected human connections that so often transform the experience of travel; those personal connections, those 600 interviews that celebrated the gifts of kindness and warmth. They restored my trust in mankind. Each unexpected gift left a lasting impression, beautifully realized in the people I met along the way. It was *the kindness of strangers* that made all the difference. It was especially noticeable through the many people who touched my life and continue their generosity and compassion to this day. I needed to honor them.

That revision allowed KRUSING AMERICA to eventually win over 60 Awards at film festivals all over the world. From Berlin to Bali, to finishing as the Overall Winner at the International Tourism Awards, the Festival Winner at the Directors Awards, and concluding with the ultimate privilege of winning both Film-maker of the Year and Director of the Year.

Despite every challenge, I don't have any regrets for choosing this road. I'm amazed at how it has grown into something I could never have imagined. After starting off as a documentary film, it's now a completed, ready-to-air TV docu-series with the potential of a Season Two featuring a whole different family in different circumstances, who discover *their* home through the kindness of strangers.

I'm not sure what the next step in the journey of KRUSING AMERICA, and for me, will be. But at this point, I'm planning on one thing only . . . I'm planning to be surprised.

We must let go of the life we have planned, so as to accept the one that is waiting for us.

–Joseph Campbell

As a News Correspondent, International Spokesperson, and multi-award winning Documentarian, LINDA KRUSE has written, produced, and directed projects worldwide that explore challenging and intriguing topics while definitively capturing real people and the worlds they live in. Linda's work is always presented with a creative elegance that reflects her signature style.

www.lindakruse.com

Team Building, Leadership, and My Brother's Murder

By Lynette Louise

I have always been an entrepreneur. As a child, I caught and sold catfish that my friends purchased and proudly placed in their bathtubs, unbeknownst to their parents. I ate worms for a quarter, put on plays for a nickel, sold bullfrogs for a dime, read palms for a dollar, arm wrestled the boys for fifty cents. Eventually I discovered babysitting, my main occupation from age twelve till I left home at fifteen.

I was also a leader. The two go nicely together. I performed thought provoking puppet shows at age five, sermons and plays with a call to action by ages eight and nine, organized sit-ins for the right to wear jeans, and refused to join groups that infused slave like obedience from its members. People loved or hated me depending on my age, the subject matter; the inconvenience caused. They emulated me or tried to squash me depending on the degree to which I was an affront to their way of thinking. I was always a leader.

Though I didn't always know what to do with people.

One day after performing in a self-penned comedy production a famous comedian shared his thoughts with me. "You're not being good to your people. The cast aren't tools, they're team mates. They have a lot to bring to the table. Let them." He was right.

Team playing was something I grappled with possibly because, as a child, helping myself was more successful than asking for help. At home I didn't lead, I distracted. I drew attention so that my siblings could escape. This was often life saving for my adopted Indian (not *Native American,* nobody called them that yet) brother. I protected him from being beaten whenever I could.

One year I couldn't.

I had grown up and moved. I was not available to block the fists. That beating was from a friend who—despite the cries for mercy—pushed my brother off a third story balcony. I was his emergency contact. When the police came to find me, I was gone. He lay in a coma and then he died, alone.

I am a woman of action, someone who takes care of things and people. I could no longer take care of my brother's life so I tried to take care of his death.

My father said he couldn't afford the burial. I went to the nearest church and arranged to have my brother's body 'handled' free. En route to the graveyard, my father intercepted the body. Everyone yelled at me. I was stumbling around, trying to do something, blinded by anger and hate. I went to the police, unannounced. On the desk, I saw pictures of my brother's bloody face in my peripheries but I couldn't look at them. The officer promised to inform me on court proceedings, but didn't. The murderer got four years.

I was a mess, useless, un-leader-like. I went on the radio to scream injustice and blithered like an idiot-sister no one could listen to. I wrote offensive articles about his humanness that no one would publish. The harder I tried to be a woman of action taking care of my brother's death the less effective I became. I made messes, hurt his memory trying to help it, saw myself in the mirror, screaming and smashing my house.

I needed help, my passion was too big, my pain too angry.

Help was something being a child of abuse hadn't taught me to accept. Help hurt. Protection was only ever gotten by being in action. My brother, who was just an adopted Indian that wouldn't turn white even when you washed him up, and dressed him in a fortrell suit, was abused, both before and after we got him. I was angry and now he was dead and I was breaking things.

Suddenly, I understood. My passion was the problem. Passion fuels action but it also gets in the way. It blinds people. That is why we need a team of objective experts: lawyers to talk to the police, journalists to write the story, radio hosts to spread the message.

We leaders need teams because we are passionate about something. If you are a leader you are a force to be reckoned with but your vision is so focused it cannot see. Since you are an action taker you will make mistakes, you will be bullheaded, you will wish to not be distracted by details. With a good team that you treat as equals, that you converse with and listen to and reward as equals, these traits will be good traits. Teams fill in the gaps and help you stay on track. Together you will succeed. This is what my brother's murder taught me: I can't do it alone.

And so, I honor his death by respecting my team and loving the people I lead. His death changed me into someone that would never again sell catfish to a child whose mother would spank them for buying it.

After my brother's murder, I became an entrepreneur with a twist: I became a person who leads and makes money without sacrificing anyone. A person who cares about the people they serve more than about the products they sell. A person who wants to make money but has no desire to make ALL the money. A person who will only bring into the world products and services that help, even when that is a poor marketing choice.

Because of my brother's murder, I am a leader who holds hands and walks with their team rather than ahead of them. I do this as a global therapist, an author, a speaker and more. In the end humanity gained from my brother's murder. We are a team. We walk together. And that is how we grow, wonderful to behold.

Still, if I could change anything, it would be the day I let go of my brother's hand.

I love you Henry.

Lynette Louise (The Brain Broad) is a renowned international mental health expert, award-winning author, speaker, and performer.

She advises people of influence on how to effectively optimize performance in the workplace. She changes brain habits and behaviors globally, improving corporate cognition and mental health for families with disabilities.

www.lynettelouise.com

Turning Pain into Purpose

By Ellen Marrs

On Thanksgiving Day in 1982, my mother died of colon cancer at the young age of 38. She left behind a husband and three children. On the afternoon of my mother's funeral, we returned home to find my father's girlfriend, and her children, moving into our home. This was a complete shock. We didn't know he had a girlfriend during the remaining months of my mother's life. It was worse because the woman was my mother's best friend.

As I tried to process the thought of life without my mother and the "new normal" of our home, I didn't think life could get much worse. That's when my father told me that he wasn't my biological dad. He proceeded to share the details of how he met my mother when she was pregnant with me. He informed me that I was the product of my mother's affair with a married man. The very thought of this shattered my world, but also explained a side of my life that no one knew. I had been abused for many years by the man who I thought was my father. After learning that I wasn't his daughter, I realized that this must have been why he treated me so differently from my sister, who was his biological child.

Within months of my mother's passing, I was told that we were going to visit family members who lived about two hours away. After we arrived at their home, I was informed that my dad no longer wanted to raise me. He had tried to find someone to take me in, but no one would. It was at this moment that I started to believe the lie that I was not wanted. With no forewarning, I was left standing on the porch as my father pulled away with my sister in the car. My world was rocked. I would never go home again. In just a few short months, I had lost my mother, my home, the only family I ever knew and ultimately, my self-esteem. It was on this day that I began my journey of questioning the reason that trials and difficult circumstances seemed to be an on-going part of my life.

Fortunately, I was given a new life with a family who loved me as their own. However, I still carried the feeling of abandonment and worthlessness deep within my soul. This feeling of lack caused my relationships to suffer and kept me "on guard" with others. I vowed never to be harmed or abandoned again. Although I maintained a tough exterior, I constantly questioned why God would ever let such terrible things happen to me. Why would He allow me to be born if I was going to be treated so poorly as a child and left on someone's doorstep, like an unwanted animal? Growing up, my constant prayer was that I would someday realize the purpose of the pain that I had experienced at such a young age.

Beginning in 2011, I started to see the reason for my difficult childhood when my husband and I made the choice to raise someone else's children as our own. Rick and I became foster parents for the state of Arizona. We cared for two young boys for two years before they were returned to their biological family. As much as we grieved their departure, we knew that being reconciled with their family was all in God's plan. We were blessed to be part of their story and we still celebrate the small (and large) victories that we had with them.

Our next foster care placement of two girls began a journey for which we could have never planned. Upon learning that the girls had two other siblings elsewhere, we decided to make it our mission to reunite these children and find an adoptive home for all four of them together. This turned out to be much more difficult than we thought. As months passed, we were unable to find a family that would adopt all four children, especially because of the special needs involved. That's when an adoption worker pointed out that no one had ever fought for these children like we had.

After much prayer and discussion, we signed our intent to adopt all four children. Ironically, I was eight and a half months pregnant at the time. With this adoption, we would be growing our family from four to nine people in just nine short months. On my birthday in 2014, I woke up with a newborn on my chest and four new members in our family. I was overwhelmed, to say the least. I was trying to bond with five children, all five years old and younger, at the same time.

During those nine months, we made space in our home for the five newest members on "Planet Marrs". We constructed bunk beds, bought a larger vehicle, worked with counselors, lawyers, adoption workers, case managers, and many other people involved in the process. Finally in November, we officially became the Marrs family of nine.

It has not been an easy process, but it has definitely been rewarding. I have seen my own past circumstances come back to help me in understanding some of the behaviors and actions of our adopted children. I can relate, in many ways, to things that they do and say. If it hadn't been for my own difficult childhood, I wouldn't be able to think through some of the solutions that we have found for our children.

Although we still have difficult days, primarily because of our children's past, I can now say that I've been able to use my own past to help change the lives of four children who might not have been reunited otherwise. I also use the details of my journey to help other abuse victims, foster children, and potential foster/ adoptive parents. I now realize the purpose for my pain and I use it to help others and glorify God.

Ellen is an entrepreneur, homeschooling mom of seven, motivational speaker, marathoner, and mentor to foster and adoptive families. She is the author of "Lessons from the Finish Line", her personal story of faith, passion, and perseverance. Ellen teaches individuals and organizations the importance of expressing gratitude through her business, as well as her class, "Gratitude: The Missing Link". She was recently featured in Networking Times magazine, a global publication for the network marketing profession.

www.ellenmarrs.com

Attitude Is Everything

An Adventure in Breast Cancer

By Debbie McCormick

It was the spring of 2011. I happily made my annual pilgrimage to the Breast Imaging Center in Orange, CA for a mammogram. Soon after, I was notified that they wanted to do a follow-up ultrasound.

I'd received these notifications after my mammograms many times before. No matter how flat the mammogram machine tried to pancake my breasts, or how loudly I squealed, sometimes the radiologists just wanted a closer look before saying, "See you next year."

I wasn't at all worried that they'd find cancer. God had already hurled some pretty big obstacles at me: the death of my husband when my son was 10 months old, enduring the medical malpractice trial that followed, and the loss of nearly all my savings in the early 2000's. Surely I had earned immunity.

So when my phone rang on Tuesday, March 8, 2011, just after 8 am and I saw that it was my long-time family doctor, I answered, "To what do I owe this early-morning pleasure?"

And he said, "Hi. Um, they found cancer on the ultrasound."

"Excuse me?"

"The ultrasound shows you have breast cancer."

I can't tell you if he said anything else. I probably thanked him for calling. I just sat there . . . then burst into tears. CANCER. The concept was so big the inside of my head echoed. I wasn't told how big or how far along the tumor was.

I must have been a freaking serial killer in a past life to deserve this.

I called my mom, a sturdy age 89 at the time. I don't know what I said, but she cried too. "We'll get through this."

How?

I literally made a list of everything I'd ever done that I was proud of, anything that showed I could accomplish something difficult. Like when I was 17, I memorized a 90-minute speech and gave it flawlessly. I didn't trip going down steep stairs in my floor-length wedding dress the day I got married (hey, everything was fair game that day). I gave birth to a 9-pound, 9-ounce baby. Vaginally. I started to gain confidence.

I looked up how much protection my HMO insurance provided. I discovered that the only surgeon they offered was a leg surgeon. Hmmmm. This is not good.

I remembered that the Imaging Center was part of BreastLink, one of the finest breast cancer research, oncology and surgery centers in the country. I trusted the doctors there and felt strongly that working with them would bring me the best possible outcome. Unfortunately, they didn't accept my HMO, so I started researching PPOs. Cigna was accepted by all my doctors, but their new-patient acceptance period didn't start until June 1st, 2011, three months from then.

By this time, I'd met with the head of radiology at the Imaging Center, and the news was mostly good: there were four spots that we'd caught very early, and they were non-aggressive (slow-growing). YESSSS! (I'm pretty sure I fist-pumped that bit of news while rocketing out of my chair and doing the Happy Dance, but my memory isn't entirely clear.)

The bad news was that not only were the tumors not close together, they weren't even in just one breast. No lumpectomies were possible; I had to lose both breasts.

Then came a blessing. After explaining my insurance situation to one of BreastLink's outstanding surgeons, he assured me I could safely postpone surgery until I could be covered under Cigna, and he would do the operation. Yet another blessing: the brand new Affordable Care Act prevented Cigna from denying me coverage for a pre-existing condition. No leg surgeon! Woohoo!

When I finally sat down to process, I experienced awe (this was BIG) then grief (the body I was born with would never again be the same).

I started forming a response to that negative news that I use to this day. I call it the "Well, look at it this way" attitude.

After I had fully grieved, I thought, "Well, look at it this way: after months of breast feeding many moons ago, the Girls never did bounce back (so to speak) to their original glory. Actually, this is great! I'm gonna get a perky new set!"

I absorbed that attitude into my bones. I was determined that this surgery was going to come out a Win for me. I couldn't have a recurrence because no original breast tissue would remain, and I was going to get a brand new set of twins! I joked with my girlfriends that my thighs might be 50 but my Girls would look 20. I was going to do this thing with all the humor and grace I had.

My mom was another huge blessing. She worked off her anxiety about my illness by going into Nurse Mode. She said a temporary goodbye to her weekly canasta games and moved into my house, helping me with my twice-daily surgery drainage, doing the laundry, making our meals and making sure her grandson got to his basketball games. I was happily high on painkillers the whole time, so I caused her no trouble. Though even as adults, we weren't strangers to mother/daughter angst, we drew closer through our shared goal.

The biggest gift came in the form of a decision: I took this on as a second chance to create a life I loved. From then on I would live with joy and gratitude. No more "I can't." I would start a business I loved, one that would help others and give me financial independence. I would become an activist for the causes I believed would make the world a better place. I began a spiritual practice that sustains me to this day.

I've been cancer-free since that 2011 surgery. My son is about to graduate from college and frequently comes by to enjoy the one meal I know how to cook. I know my dear mom watches over me still, having passed away in 2015 at the age of 93.

I am truly blessed.

Debbie McCormick is a LinkedIn trainer, speaker, and author of the Amazon #1 best-seller The LinkedIn Manual for Rookies. *Her online courses teach business people, from beginners to advanced users, how to easily attract, connect to, and do business with their ideal clients.*

www.DebbieMcCormick.com

I Had to Fall Down before I Got Up

By Siobhan McKenna
Aerospace Engineer, Author & Speaker

Mission Statement

To inspire and empower women around the world to design and build extraordinary lives.

> "As I bruised my knees and at times, felt like I was trudging through mud, I endeared somehow, someway. That may sound nebulous, even I am still figuring it out. "
>
> —Siobhan McKenna

Our Goal

Empowering Women (Inside/Out)

My Success Story

Sometimes in life we have all heard life can throw us curveballs. Well, ain't that just grand. I got tired of the curveballs. My story, I had done everything right (as expected) with unknown blips. College degrees, successful career, married, warm safe loving home, lean trim body, wonderful friends, and family.

And then I **Collapsed**!

Right in downtown Calabasas, California. Yes sir-ree. How embarrassing. I was literally living on fumes. Meaning driving up to Los Angeles from San Diego without any fuel in my body. Bottom line, I completely lost my appetite. I had written the book "Imagineering Your Life". Now, it was time for me to read it.

Note: My friends, while visiting me in the hospital, later told me how dreamy and gorgeous the captain and lieutenant of the fire department looked. (The ones who came and lifted me off to the hospital). True friends, I will always be grateful to them, for the laughter, kindness, and caring for being in such a serious situation.

Moving Forward

Currently, I am attending a graduate program at UCSD in Systems Engineering. My goal is to teach and speak in universities throughout the world to empower women in STEM—Science, Technology, Engineering, and Math: Education for Global Leadership

True Story: Northeastern University, studying and majoring in Mechanical Engineering, I got a **'B'** in one class. To an overachiever like me that is unacceptable. And, I know anyone reading this book can completely relate. I approached the professor, after receiving the grade, asking him why my fellow student had received the same grades throughout the course and he received an 'A'.

I have never shared this story in writing, but now is my time to step up for all of you brilliant women.

To my astonishment, he replied, "You are female, why do you deserve an 'A'? I was speechless and dumbfounded. Eliminate self-doubt on a mission to stun the world. And most importantly be happy and share your wisdom. I sometimes ask myself, how do people do it. It is literally a Rat Race out there. Wake-up, coffee, kids, commute, work, work, work, commute, home, dinner, relationship, sleep. And, then it begins all again, the next day, day after day. Welcome to life.

What's up with that? We are so time-bound and wrapped around being successful, we lose sight of what is really important.

Question: Have you ever felt like what the 'frig' am I doing here? Please Answer: _____

True Story: Business men were travelling to Mexico on vacation. And after tasting the best taco's, they have ever had, they expressed to the owner/chef, "You have the freshest, most delicious tacos, why don't you enlarge and come to the United States. This is delicious and you can retire and have so much money. He replied, "Why? Then I can retire and fish all day. That's what I do now. And I am happy."

Point. Do what you love, forget, and disregard other people's opinions (unless, it's in your heart for some type of change).

Empower Yourselves Ladies. We are on our way.

Lots of Love on your wonderful empowering journey.

Siobhan McKenna

p.s. Our Goal: Empower beautiful, wonderful women around the world to Rock! And know in your heart of hearts you are Worth IT!

Now that you have heard Siobhan McKenna's story of empowering herself, and how incredibly grateful she is to be part of the fabulous book **'Women Who Rock',** check out these precious nuggets of inspiration from **Investor's Business Daily.**

IBD's (Investor's Business Daily) 10 Secrets to Success

Investor's Business Daily has spent years analyzing leaders and successful people in all walks of life.

Most have 10 traits that, when combined, can turn dreams into reality. A list is compiled from the results of thousands of case studies / biographies of what famous and successful people did to get where they are now—from Ben Franklin to Bill Gates to Mother Theresa to Babe Ruth to Martin Luther King . . . Not simply the rich, but people who truly did extraordinary things with their lives.

1. **HOW YOU THINK IS EVERYTHING**: Always be positive. Think success, not failure. Beware of a negative environment. (Put all negative thoughts and worry out of your mind—think positive—be happy).

2. **DECIDE UPON YOUR TRUE DREAMS AND GOALS**: Write down your specific goals and develop a plan to reach them. (Clearly identify what you choose in life and focus on it constantly).

3. **TAKE ACTION**: Goals are nothing without action. Don't be afraid to get started now. Just do it. (If it feels right for you, and you truly love it, jump straight into what you choose in life at this moment—move now, for time passes so quickly).

4. **NEVER STOP LEARNING**: Go back to school or read books. Get training and acquire skills. (Start now, for time passes so quickly).

5. **PERSIST AND WORK HARD**: Success is a marathon, not a sprint. Never give up. (Focus).

6. **LEARN TO ANALYZE DETAILS**: Get all the facts, all the information. Learn from your mistakes. (Also, trust your feelings, especially your first impression, for often this is true for many people).

7. **BUDGET YOUR TIME AND MONEY**: Don't let other people or things distract you. (Know your priorities—put them in writing—think about them often—move towards them).

8. **DON'T BE AFRAID TO INNOVATE**: Following the herd is a sure way to mediocrity (move into the greatest vision that you ever had about yourself—see more in yourself and others than ever before).

9. **COMMUNICATE AND DEAL WITH PEOPLE EFFEC-TIVELY**: No person is an island. Learn to understand and motivate others (and hence motivate yourself—see all people as one and have no fear).

10. **BE HONEST AND DEPENDABLE, TAKE RESPONSI-BILITY**: Otherwise, No.'s 1–9 won't matter. (Truth should always be your highest choice).

Siobhan has worked in the Aerospace and Defense industry for over seventeen years as a software and systems engineer designing and developing large complex computer systems. Along with her education and experience in this technical arena, Siobhan has been studying and modeling successful people for twenty-five years.

She is dedicated to helping people define and live their ultimate lives. Siobhan has had a fascination with people who have been happy and ultimately live a wonderful and fulfilled life.

Siobhan is also the creator of the Imagineering Your Life System for Success, a home study course for anyone wanting to design and build extraordinary lives for themselves. Siobhan's insights are fresh and compelling.

www.ImagineeringYourLife.com

Powerful Wisdom for Everyday Living

The Gift That Keeps on Giving . . .

By Crystal Neels, MSW

It was December 15th, 2011, and I could hardly breathe. I was on my second round of antibiotics and nothing seemed to be making any difference. The Emergency Room doctor told me I had the beginnings of pneumonia and sent me home to rest.

There I sat on the edge of my bed at 10pm, fully dressed in my winter jacket, scarf, turtle neck, sweat suit, and knee high socks trembling from head to toe. I was freezing and sweating at the same time and had no idea how to manage this beast of an illness, the likes of which I had never known before.

As our ten year old daughter, Emily, laid out her sleeping bag at the edge of our bed, she looked up with deep concern and asked me, "Mommy, are you going to die tonight?" My heart broke as I struggled to muster the strength not to react and said, "No, honey, I am not going to die. God is not finished with me yet. I have a lot to do."

In that moment, I had the scariest thought. What if this was my last night on the planet? What kind of legacy had I passed on to my children, Seth, Nicholas and Emily, if this was my last night of being alive? I began to think about all the lessons I had learned in life that I hadn't yet shared with them.

Suddenly, I was so exhausted. I leaned back to go to sleep and at that very moment, I heard a commanding voice. The voice said,

"Get up." I looked around the room and thought to myself, "I must be running a really high fever." A few moments later, the voice again said, "Get up." This time I thought, "I'm must be REALLY out of it. I'm hearing voices." The third time, the commanding voice said, "Get up and go to the computer NOW!"

I couldn't imagine getting up. It took everything I had to get out of bed. My body broke into a cold sweat and with my knees knocking and a fever raging, I sat down at the computer. As I began to write, I suddenly experienced the most amazing clarity and healing that I have ever known. My fingers began to fly across the keyboard capturing pearls of wisdom and lessons for life page after page, hour after hour into the night. It felt as if God was speaking right through me.

At the same time, I experienced an exhilarating flood of love, joy, peace and understanding. This book seemed to write itself that evening.

As I began to share my experience and writing with the people in my life, most of my friends, family, and colleagues were struck by the clarity and power of the material. Many of them were moved to tears. Others pointed to the Biblical nature of each lesson. Some found direction in the challenges they were dealing with. Others experienced healing in their relationships. All of them wanted to know more.

Over time, it became clear to me that each of these lessons for life were divinely inspired. Through prayer, I was led to identify the scripture that sourced each lesson for life in this book. I came to understand that this book was written not only for my children but for all of us as God's children.

In the process, I learned that if we really trust, we will experience things we have never experienced before. If we really listen, we will hear things we have never heard before. If we really look, we will see things we have never seen before, all of which deepens our capacity to be all that we can be.

We have all been given a voice and it's time to use it to make a difference.

This book is written for people who are looking to elevate who they are, in service of who they can be. It is a gift that keeps on giving and it is an honor to be the messenger.

Get ready to grow exponentially.

Crystal Neels, MSW is an accomplished author, trainer, and speaker, well-known for delivering inspiring seminars and quality education that make a profound impact in the world. Her compelling message is both relevant and far-reaching. Her book and consulting programs are stimulating and provocative and consistently exceed people's expectations.

www.powerfulwisdomforeverydayliving.com

Don't Be Afraid to Ask

By Kathy Pendleton

I'm launching a business. It's a mind-boggling, character-expanding endeavor that has occupied my mind and my heart for a number of years. The business idea began over six years ago. The experiences that led me down this path began more than thirty years before that.

When I was twenty-eight years old, my 50-year-old mom suddenly passed away. I got the call on Labor Day afternoon in my newly-purchased Florida condo that I was eager for her to see. It was truly incomprehensible, we didn't have any idea that she was seriously ill and neither did she. I asked what had happened, asked everyone, collected many details, and spoke for hours with my aunt, a doctor. Mom's condition was obviously more serious than we had known and the medication, coupled with her activities (boating on a very hot, summer day on the Chesapeake Bay) probably created the fatal conditions that led to her death.

In the weeks that followed, I reviewed the details over and over in my mind. She was under a doctor's care. Didn't she ask about her condition, the medication, side effects, or things not to do? Didn't the doctor or the pharmacist discuss any of that information? It all preyed on my mind. I agonized and analyzed and it took six months for me to stop crying during the drive to and from work, but eventually I moved on without resolving any of my questions.

As life continued, my pre-occupation with health care issues grew. I worked with a nurse, who opened my eyes to her point of view: that of a patient-focused, licensed medical professional. I expanded my horizons further when I attempted to use the health care system in a couple of foreign countries, once with their health insurance, once without—WITH is definitely better! Did you realize that your U.S. health insurance is good only in the U.S.?

I formed opinions about incidents that happened in my own medical treatment. Have you ever been in an examining room discussing your condition with the doctor, when a nurse knocked on the door to ask the doctor something? The doctor left the room. After a few minutes the nurse returned and told me to get dressed, that the appointment was over. What? Ok, it only happened once. It only recently occurred to me that she probably used that ruse to get out of an appointment that was running too long.

Years passed and some family members became seriously ill. I listened, observed, questioned. I formed opinions about what went well and what didn't. I didn't approve of the fact that nobody seemed to do anything when my mother-in-law got to her hospital room after surgery and there was no pain medication for her. I was also dissatisfied when my father-in-law had a stroke in his hospital room on a Saturday morning, and when I arrived nothing was happening—no lights, no crowd of doctors, nothing.

Finally, I took some action. I knew how to reach one of his doctors and I made the call. The doctor arrived within a couple of hours and brought a neurologist with him. During my father-in-law's illness, there was so much happening that I didn't understand, I assembled my own "team"—friends and relatives who were part of the medical system. I asked questions of my "team", as well as the nurses and doctors, and an idea began to form that the information I was learning would be helpful to anybody in my situation.

Unfortunately, I was still angry about these incidents. Wouldn't you be angry if you saw your mom whimpering in pain and no one was doing anything to relieve it? Wouldn't you be angry if you found your father-in-law alone, expressionless, and unable to speak, and then found out that your mother-in-law hadn't been called? And the anger was what came across most clearly during my conversations. I worked with a speaking coach to develop my talk, but the anger remained. Not compassion or concern or knowledge—mostly anger.

So, I worked on myself to uncover the compassion and fear behind my anger. I wanted to be able to relate to the frustration we feel when we leave a doctor's office more confused and fearful than when we entered, because our questions weren't answered. I wanted to understand a family's continuing uncertainty over a treatment decision that ultimately didn't help and led to suffering. My introspection took a few years and it led to a calmness and determination. Then again, I still become angry when incidents happen like those mentioned above. Now, though, the anger sits behind the fear and sadness of family members like me, who are trying to make decisions about health care with incomplete information.

So now we arrive at the present and I'm ready to launch the business. It's called Get the Care You Deserve. My mission is to teach people like me, with family members who need medical experts, treatment, and hospitalizations, how to step up and:

1. have the courage and the confidence to ask for answers and options.
2. get a second and third opinion.
3. repeat tests if you feel it's necessary.
4. make the decision with the knowledge and understanding gained.
5. ask questions to understand about the care and treatment in a medical facility.

Get the Care You Deserve also teaches family members to pay attention to the treatment in a hospital or rehab center because errors happen every day. We can learn to trust our intuition and knowledge of our own bodies to discern when we should press ahead and be assertive, so we get the best for our sick or injured loved one. We can learn about our own illnesses, conditions, and treatments, so that we recognize recovery, reactions, and sometimes limitations in our own bodies. This awareness might have helped my mom all those years ago.

We can do this. And as we do this, we can change the look and feel of medical care in the future, for ourselves and our children. We can create a new and better way, in which patients participate with their doctors in choosing a treatment option that's right for the patient and their family.

After many years as a technical trainer with various computer software companies, Kathy has directed her analytical fervor toward managing our own health care. Her fifteen years of helping family members have created her passion for avoiding hospital mistakes and patient participation in treatment decisions.

www.GetTheCareYouDeserve.com

Get Your Foot in the Door!

By Roberta Perry

"She can't type, she can't take shorthand . . . but she can keep your department organized!"

Helen was right on all three counts, although she wouldn't really know how right until she'd seen me spin my stuff. She was Office Manager at Stuart Anderson's Restaurants headquarters in Seattle and I had just interviewed with her for the role of Secretary to the Director of Entertainment. A Master's degree and dreams of teaching for a living just weren't enough, so I was starting at the beginning—on the ground floor in business—as a secretary.

Three days after joining the organization, Stuart called me into his office to welcome me to the company. We chatted about the challenges women face in business, especially the restaurant business. He highly recommended that I go down the street and join a local Toastmasters club (www.toastmasters.org). His challenge was to join up and *just say yes* to every opportunity—which actually meant—volunteer for any communication/leadership role.

So I did.

I will never forget my first Toastmasters meeting. The group had only admitted females for seven months when I walked through the doors. There I was—27 men and me, the 5 foot, 3 ½ inch blonde. Toastmasters and I have had a love affair ever since, but that's a story for another time.

Success in business rarely comes in a flash. It was a year before I had created a couple of major wins that pulled me out of the secretaries' cafeteria and landed me in the "reservations-only", lunch hotspots with corporate management. There was the first book of menus for the restaurant chain. And later, hosting a series of VIP tours on a 52-foot yacht.

During that year I learned a lot from Stuart—what it means to do your best regardless, to always stand by your beliefs, and to function as a true team.

In 1980, the Entertainment Director resigned. Stuart encouraged me to pitch myself to the Board of Directors as his replacement. It was a bit of a tough sell. At the time, we had 50 plus restaurants scattered across 20 states. The Entertainment Department was responsible for the nightclub and bar, live entertainment, promotions, and marketing campaigns. In those days there were concerns over whether a woman had the muscle to effectively and safely run a liquor-based business, interviewing bands, being in bars late at night, and travelling alone.

Nevertheless, I went before the board and pitched. A consensus emerged. "Let her fill the role for two months—we'll see if she can handle the job." Two months later, Stuart threw the party he had promised if the Board green-lighted my permanent placement in the role.

Congrats! I was the Entertainment Director for a major American restaurant chain. Too bad the business was losing money. The 175-seat bars were fun but not profitable, and it fell to me to reverse the trend. We were known for our live entertainment/bands—Rock n' Roll with a splash of country—but society was sliding into the disco era. Embracing what that trend might mean to us, I attended a Billboard convention in NY. After listening to a seminar on managing a disco and DJ's, I managed to ask the wrong people the right questions, took the laughs and ridicule on the chin, sought out the right people, proposed ideas back and forth, cast a wide talent net, and put together a 300 person team of disco DJ's and supporting personnel to take our entertainment business to the next level.

And take it to the next level we did.

Progress in the fast-moving entertainment business requires foresight, the ability to cut to the final scene quickly, and the brass to be certain you are right when you do it. For example, early on in Dallas it became apparent we needed a new Audio/Lighting company for the bars. The nationwide search narrowed to two companies. In the final bake-off I asked only one question . . . "What is the future of the nightclub business?" One company gave me a new disco ball! The other company headed up by "futurist" Brian Edwards said, "We'll put a remote 10 by 10 screen on that wall there because there is something coming down the road called music videos."

We hired him. The first two music videos were a hit in the pilot site. We re-modelled the remaining sites and we were off and running in the profitable disco age.

The years with Stuart Anderson were fantastic. In January 1984, I decided I'd been a road warrior long enough. Brian Edwards and I launched Edwards Technologies, Inc., and later a division called "ETI Music Video Network". These were exciting times. During the next few years I had the pleasure of being president of ETV, providing nightclubs and bars with music videos. It was also my pleasure to be the second President of the Nightclub and Bar Association during those formative years.

Looking back over this time I learned several important lessons that have helped shape my career:

1. Find a mentor and be a mentor! There's no substitute for experienced counsel, the ability to listen and understand, and the willingness to let you solve your own challenges.
2. Be yourself! Don't try to be them. Trust me I know from experience—I even tried wearing bow ties.
3. Get your foot in the door. Just start somewhere and figure it out from there. As Les Brown said, "Shoot for the Moon . . . and if you miss you will still be among the stars."

And finally, to all you women with the brass to get out there, to mix it up, to push forward despite reasons not to, to keep working towards your dreams—you ROCK!

"Roberta Perry is a Business Development specialist. She has served as Chairman of the Nightclub and Bar Association; as President of

the Themed Entertainment Association; sat on Seattle Fair Campaign and Practices Commission; International Board Director for Toastmasters International, and currently serves on the Board for Lawrence Anthony's Earth Organization."

www.RobertaPerry.com

Blessings

By B Heather Pinard

I am dying: my body is giving out. It cannot go any further. The doctors don't give me much of a chance. A wheelchair is in my future, at best. At worse, the drugs they want me on will cause liver and kidney failure in 3 1/2 years. Tylenol and other over the counter drugs do not even make a dent in the excruciating pain I am in. I want to just crawl in bed, pull the covers up, and give up on life. Then I remember I am in pain lying down too.

It all started when I was 5. First I was molested and at 6 I was excited to go to a new school. Unfortunately, I was bullied, taunted, and teased in school causing me much mental anguish. While on a trip with my family, I became very ill. I was more susceptible to viruses and bacteria because of the trauma inflicted on me for so many years. My immune system was compromised. All my joints were inflamed and moving them felt like daggers and arrows piercing my whole body. Every other week, I would come down with a bad sore throat. Nothing they were doing for me made it better. My tonsils were removed thinking that would solve the problem. The whole process scared me. They made me walk into the room the surgery was taking place and sit in a chair that reminded me of an electric chair. As if that was not bad enough, they tied me down and then they put a mask over my face which I fought against as hard as I could—I was terrified. With all that exertion, I could not hold my breath any longer and began to breathe in deeply. After the operation, they would not let me go home unless I ate ice cream. Most of the time I would love ice cream—this time it hurt to swallow.

When the removal of my tonsils did not stop the problem, they realized there was more to it. After they finally diagnosed the illness, the course of treatment was complete bedrest for 9 months, penicillin for the rest of my life, and steroids for 6 months. The doctor would come every week and take vials and vials of my blood. I thought he was going to drain me dry. As long as I looked away when he would draw my blood, I was fine. I began to feel like a pin cushion. My mother had to exercise my legs so that I would not get atrophy. Even so, I had to learn to walk all over again.

The drugs they had put me on helped me get rid of the inflammation and in the process, they caused other challenges: my back grew to create a double curve and caused one hip to be higher than the other, keeping me off balance. During the day when I was up and about like a normal 11-year-old, I was concentrating on other aspects of my life and as long I kept moving, I felt alright. As I would lay down to go to sleep at night I would be in such agony that in order to sleep at night, I had to teach myself how to relax only one joint at a time. I would start at the top of my head and work my way down to my feet where I would relax each joint in my toes and then work back up my body. Some nights I would have to do it 3 times before I could relax enough go to sleep.

My life continued like this for 35 years. I had used acupuncturist, chiropractors, all to no avail. My husband would feel so sad when we would go for drives as I could not sit still for very long. I looked to not complain as we thought there was nothing to be done for the pain.

As I was given my choices of a wheelchair or drugs, I decided to go see my grandchild to mull it over. On the way there, an energy product was introduced to me that gave me significant improvement and hope that at last, I had found something that would make a difference. Within 2 weeks, I had some strength back in my arm that had stopped working, and by the year's end my joints were on track to where I did not hurt any more. At the same time, I was diagnosed with "the little c." After many biopsies, someone reminded me to have a blessing. During the blessing, I was told that if I "Give it to God" I would be fine. So I did and also did my part. I took natural products, thought of "Pacman" eating it up and spitting it out, and at my next biopsy, I was told "the little c" was gone. And as of this writing, it has been gone 21 yrs.

In those years, I thought to pass my blessings forward and I have helped thousands of people improve their quality of life. I learned more about these energy medicine products as well as different modalities to help people work through their traumas. I learned it was all about our mental attitude, even more so our thoughts and how we are influenced by the world and the people around us. Being traumatized as a youth, my subconscious was taking it all in and had created a heart wall to protect me from those stinging words. As an adult, this heart wall was keeping me stuck. I learned to release the heart wall from myself and others. I have my own practice now and teach, coach, and mentor people on their heart walls and thought processes that can harm them. I have been published twice about thoughts, words, and phrases that can make us or break us. These can be found by contacting me at heather@wordsthatkillbook.com.

B Heather Pinard graduated magna cum laude with her Master's in Education. Heather's whole life has been a journey of new discoveries and how she can make a meaningful change to the people she is coaching, teaching, or speaking with. She received a grant from the National Endowments of Art where she taught incarcerated children how to become more creative. She has had several shows and is now a Best-Selling Author where she co-authored a book with Adam Markel of New Peaks. She has her own book called "Words that Kill, the Power of Language and the Promise of Peace." She has studied with such greats as Bob Proctor of the Secret, Zig Ziegler, and many others. She is certified in applied kinesiology, healing hand/reiki, and is a certified Emotion Code practitioner. She uses her skills to make a difference in other's lives.

www.wordsthatkillbook.com

Against All Odds

By Diane Polnow

For every adversity, a seed of equal or greater benefit has been planted.

–Napolean Hill

I grew up in a small town northwest of Chicago, Illinois called Woodstock. At a young age, I found out I was adopted. My adoptive father passed away from a massive heart attack on-the-job one month after his 50th birthday. I was 17 years old when I lost him, and then my adoptive mother passed away 6 years later of cancer. Early in life, adversity struck and I was forced to raise myself financially, emotionally, mentally, and physically.

I was passionate and curious about being adopted. For years, I expressed the desire to find my birthmother, yet my adoptive mother told me she never wanted me to look for her as long as she was alive—so I obeyed. I always wondered who my birthparents were, what they looked like, what medical issues ran in the family if any, and of course, I dreamed of meeting them some day.

After my adoptive mother passed, I initiated the search for my birthmother. The adoption agency found her and tried to connect but she was not interested. I let time pass, then I tried to connect with her directly. Once again, she had no desire to meet. In the search for my birthmother, I discovered I had a half-sister so I tried to connect with her. She disappointingly was also not interested. The continued rejection hurt—and hurt deeply. It caused me to investigate into the reasons people have children. I became passionate about educating people on the financial, emotional, mental, physical, and relational realities of parenthood whether they birthed a child or otherwise so I wrote my first book, while working full time, called "**Baby Debate**: *Everything you need to consider BEFORE becoming a parent.*" I've done speaking and media as part of my teaching.

Because I knew I needed to survive on my own, making money was important to me. To me, money represented security and would allow me to have a comfortable lifestyle. It was critical to have financial health and put to use the invaluable work ethic my parents taught me. I knew I needed to select jobs that paid well, plus I learned and was schooled to build multiple streams of income.

Most of my career, I worked for Fortune 100 companies accumulating over 20 years of experience as a top performing sales leader. I built a track record of taking low performing teams to the very top, earning multiple Presidents Club awards and leading the ranking reports year after year. It wasn't easy. Throughout my career, I reported to a multitude of sales executives, was involved in multiple company reorganizations, and a company merger. In spite of all the adversity, I continued to excel, persevere, and strive for excellence. I knew if I helped others achieve their goals I would achieve mine.

I decided after my successful long-term corporate career it was time to take a break. All my years of hard work and effort in corporate paid off because it allowed me the ability to build financial health and a savings account to follow my dreams and passions.

First, I followed my passion for travel and have been blessed to travel 16 countries over the years—mostly in Europe. I loved every second of it and accumulated priceless experiences, memories, and dear life-long friends along the way.

Next, I followed my passion of having my own business. I packaged all the knowledge and experience my corporate career gave me and launched **Elite Sales Leaders**—a Consulting, Coaching, and Training company and authored my second book titled "**7**

Secrets of Building Elite Sales Teams: *Proven Ways to Increase Sales Results—For Sales Managers and Sales Executives."* I now teach my leadership success formula to corporations, entrepreneurs, and individuals to help them achieve personal and financial success so they can do things in life they've always dreamed of.

Lastly, I had always wanted an online business that would generate additional income anywhere I was, so I launched an online business called www.EuropeanDesignerLingerie.com, selling sophisticated European lingerie brands. I wanted to bring beautiful pieces Europe had to offer to the United States.

In spite of the challenges I faced at a young age, I continued to persist and strive for excellence translating into great success in my professional career. Losing my parents at an early age taught me to live life while you can—while you're here—and to do the things you want to do.

If a gal who was raised in a small town in the Midwest and forced to survive on her own can travel the world, have a successful career, be debt-free, author two books, take two years off, launch three companies, and live on the beach—you can too. Put your goals in front of you, decide what things you're passionate about doing and find a way to make them happen. Don't let challenges, obstacles, or others tell you that it cannot be done.

Do more of what makes you happy and pursue the things in life that you've always wanted to do!

Here's to your success. I'll see you at the top!

Diane Polnow is the Owner of Elite Sales Leaders, an international consulting, coaching, training company which specializes in teaching Sales Management and Sales Executives to build top performing sales teams across the globe.

Diane has a track record of taking low performing teams to the top and is an expert at driving sales results at some of the most recognizable Fortune 100 companies such as American Express and Sprint.

www.EliteSalesLeaders.com

Enough

By Veronica Centasso Pranzo

I clearly remember the day I decided the English language was not for me. . . .

I was in second grade. My classroom was on the second floor of this beautiful Venetian palace in Venice, Italy. It was about an eight minute walk from my home to school and I loved the short walk. Just one turn right, three left, a bridge and . . . well grandma was the one to bring me to school at that time, and most mornings we were stopping first at the coffee shop for her morning espresso, then to buy the newspaper and cigarettes. Grandma Luciana eventually stopped smoking later on. She stopped the day after my grandpa had heart surgery. Nevertheless, she died of lung cancer in 2012. But let's get back to my elementary school.

My classroom was the best in the building. It had this amazing fresco on the ceiling: a blue sky with soft pinkish and yellowish clouds and chubby cherubs that were looking down on us kids. I always loved angels and I loved the idea that baby angels were kind of coming to school like us and with us. I adored my teacher too. It was a private school run by nuns. "My" nun was Sr. Gabriella and I always thought she was pretty awesome. She was at my wedding and she is still my friend on Facebook today after 36 years and she actually did not kill me when I decided not to baptize my daughter. In that school, the only teacher that was not a nun was Miss Cristina, a British lady that had the pleasure to teach a foreign language to we smart little brains. One day, Miss Cristina asked me to read out loud to the class a short passage from my English book. That is when it happened! I came across the word "ENOUGH" and it was a hard word for me. What was the right pronunciation? When Miss Cristina rescued me saying that the right pronunciation was "Een'uhf", I remember looking back to the word and thinking: "What a tricky silly language! They write one thing and they read something completely different."

At that point, I was a full 7 years old, a proud Venetian! Completely at peace with the idea of NOT to having to learn a second language. Who needed English? When in my Italian, no wait, Venetian life will I ever need to speak English? And speaking of which, let's add, I did not want to have a driver's license either! You might ask: what is the connection? Well, I do not know but I remember that was the next important decision. No car for me! Cars were/are a dangerous matter. You can kill somebody, you can get killed so . . . the decision was made. And for the rest of my scholastic life, I was a brilliant student. I studied Latin, Greek and philosophy . . . I just always struggled with a foreign language because literally, at school, I had had . . . ENOUGH, and until I was 24 years old, I was convinced that if I needed it, public transportation was the answer.

I can imagine some of the theories "experts" could express: well, this is the typical example of a spoiled kid giving up at the first sign of a difficult encounter, and not wanting to drive a car is her refusal to take responsibility . . . and blah blah blah. Or?

I was six when they discover an anomaly on my spine. Doctors said that I could never do any kind of sport; I could not lift any kind of weight, not even my school backpack. Hiking was out of question, too . . . The list went on until I had ENOUGH and decided that my desire to become a ballerina was stronger. I enter a ballet company at 18 years old.

I was between six and seven when I realized that something was wrong in my family. I always have had an amazing, loving family but Mom start to cry a lot, and Grandma did too, and my uncle who was like my brother and only 13 years older than me, started acting strange . . . I loved him a lot. So many times, over his years as a drug addict, I tried to talk to him, to comfort him, to help him as much as I could. I cried with him. . . . Other times I threatened him, I despised him too. At one point the family had had ENOUGH of phone calls in the middle of the night, enough to have been fearful for his safety, and Grandma for sure had had enough of going out in the middle of the night looking for him, not knowing if she would find him dead or alive. After painful and drastic decisions were taken, he went to rehab. Rehab kind of worked. They cleaned him up.

He committed suicide a few years after, at age 33, not because of drugs but because he was depressed and he just had enough of his broken life.

I was 20. I was devastated. And I was left with a big question: when is enough really ENOUGH?

Today, I am a successful international event and wedding planner and designer. My mission is to make sure my clients celebrate their life's milestones in style while I take care of every little detail to make sure their event will be a celebration of a lifetime. I understand how important it is to celebrate life and how powerful it can be to be a service to people, to bring a smile to their faces and build happy memories.

Today I speak 4 languages and I have 2 driver's licenses: a French and a California one. I have a beautiful daughter that was born in the Caribbean and is fluent in 2 languages. I published my first book in English in 2015, "How to Plan and Design a Celebration of a Lifetime." I live in the USA, but I go back to my family in Venice every time I can.

So far, I learned that life is an amazing adventure: sometimes it is hard, painful, and you might think you cannot survive the hard proof in front of you, sometimes it might offer you joyful surprises, happy encounters, and the magic of love. Either way, I have not had enough yet.

Veronica Centasso Pranzo is an author, speaker, radio host, and international event planner and designer that lived and worked in three different continents. Born and raised in Venice, Italy she currently lives in Los Angeles from where she continues to craft elegant events and stylish wedding celebrations. Recently, she was called to do an event for 150 UN female delegates in New York, and one of her event designs was displayed at The Special Event Expo where attendees from 56 different countries were present.

www.LosAngelesExclusiveWeddings.com

Publishing a Book Helped Me Become a Celebrity in My Fields

By Suzy Prudden

I sold my first book to William Morrow at a cocktail party in East-hampton, Long Island, New York in the summer of 1971. That's how things were done in those days. I was talking to an editor from William Morrow about a book idea I had about toddler fitness, she liked it, and asked me if I had an outline. Of course I said yes. She said she'd pick it up on her way back to the city on Monday morning. I wrote the outline over the weekend, she picked it up Monday morning, and a week later called me with a book deal. I then called The William Morris Agency, told them who I was, that I'd just sold a book to William Morrow and needed an agent. They assigned an agent to me and it was a done deal; except for one very important ingredient. I couldn't write. But my husband could. I told him what I needed; he wrote the book and did the photos. Another very important ingredient was, it was the name, Prudden, they bought.

I'm the daughter of Bonnie Prudden, the Nation's foremost Fitness Authority and creator of The President's Council on Physical Fitness and Sports. She was a major figure in the fitness field and actually could be called "The Mother of Fitness". Joni Evans, my editor, knew this and was no fool.

In the late 60's and early 70's, I had a small fitness studio on the Upper West Side of Manhattan where I specialized in Toddler

Fitness. This was before Gymboree, Mommy and Me, and a host of other toddler programs that would spring up in the years to come.

Following my mother's lead, I, too became a leading authority in fitness. When my book came out in 1972, people who had thought I was a bit weird for teaching toddlers began to sit up and take notice. NYC schools starting calling me to find out what I was doing. It soon became clear that the children, who graduated from my school at the age of 3, were better equipped to go into nursery school. It became a pre-requisite that if you wanted to get your child into a good private nursery school, you sent him or her to me first. My students ranged in age from 15 months to 15 years.

Newspapers began contacting me; then the morning talk shows. I became a part of a children's television show on Saturday mornings: "The Patchwork Family" on CBS. Then came more book deals: Doubleday, Grosset and Dunlap, Simon & Schuster, Mac-Millan, Workman, Hay House and Harper San Francisco. And there were more TV and radio shows, and more newspapers and featured articles in magazines. I did 18 National Tours with books and being a spokesperson for products.

I had articles in The New York Times, Boston Globe, Chicago Tribune, The Washington Post, The Baltimore Sun, The Denver Post, and The Los Angeles Times, just to name a few. I was quoted in Newsweek, Vogue, People, New York Magazine, and The Wall Street Journal. I was even interviewed on the Walter Cronkite CBS news. NBC called me to do a pilot with Dr. Frank Field on health. The pilot didn't go anywhere but a producer at NBC saw it, liked me, and hired me to be the fitness expert for their show, "The Prime of your Life." I was their fitness expert with a live 7-minute segment every Sunday morning for 3 ½ years. That lead to my own morning talk show on NBC and a short stint as the "on camera" Fitness Reporter for The Today Show. I was a sought after guest on most of the major talk shows across the country. And yes, of course, I was a featured guest on The Oprah Show.

All this came from a small book published in 1972. Yes, I had the name that got me in the door, but it was up to me to stay in the room—which I did. I was able to sell my business and retire in

1983 at the age of 40 and take a few years off to play, travel, and do my Eat, Pray, Love experience. I just didn't eat much.

Being a published author positions you as an expert in your field. It gives you the opportunity to spread your message in a way that people see you as an authority. Being a published author got me speaking opportunities, endorsement opportunities, and positioned me as "The Go To" person for fitness in New York City. My list of clients was the who's who in the entertainment industry. I was one of the "Beautiful" people in New York and The Hamptons. It was an amazingly heady time. I made a lot of money, had a lot of fun, and made a difference.

It's over 30 years since I've worn a leotard and people still ask me, "Are you that Suzy Prudden?" It happened just a few weeks ago, at a conference in South Carolina.

If you have a product or a program you need to write a book. It doesn't have to be 300 pages of blood, sweat, and tears. It actually needs to be short because people today don't like to read and don't have the attention span for big, informational books. You just need to position yourself as the expert in your field. A book gives you the foundation to build a 7 figure business and puts you in the forefront of your industry. Your book is the outline for your Webinars, Tele-Classes, radio shows, YouTube tips, mini seminars, one or two or even three day seminars, retreats, certification Programs, License agreements, JV opportunities, and speaking opportunities. You are automatically positioned at the higher end of your profession and immediately garner more respect, make more money and get noticed by the media. Having a book increases your Brand Reach. A book is just the beginning.

SUZY PRUDDEN, internationally acclaimed speaker and seminar leader, author and TV/radio host and personality, has been inspiring audiences and groups since 1965. She is a NY Times Best Selling Author, fitness expert, hypnotherapist, success coach and Publisher. She is a master of self-reinvention. At 73, she is the co-creator and publisher of the Your Amazing Itty Bitty Publishing series.

Yes, you've seen her on Oprah, Good Morning America, and The Today Show.

The NY Times says, "If Suzy is talking about it today, the rest of the country will be talking about it tomorrow."

www.ittybittypublishing.com

You Are Born for More

By Neecol Resnin

I wanted to quit, but I loved the fix. I was deceived by the high. I am educated, having two master degrees, one in business and one in clinical psychology, yet I was duped by the greatest deceiver of them all: DRUGS. I would take my drugs by prescription medication, (after all, it was prescribed by a doctor), I would smoke my drugs, snort the drugs, and drink. I just needed the fix, anyway I could get it.

I share my story in hopes that it will inspire someone to make a change. Continuing drugs means a life of failure, legal brushes, and even death. It is as if drugs have a spirit. The spirit to cause addiction, the spirit to bind, the spirit to confine. You can overcome no matter how many times you have tried. You are worth it.

Drugs are a great distractor, a great deceiver. One can be grand and on top of the world without ever leaving a bed or couch. Drugs are an equal-opportunity employer. One can spend hundreds of thousands of dollars to be an employee. One can turn over the weekly paycheck to drugs. It is OK whatever the arrangement is; in the end, drugs win.

I was deceived and became an employee of Use Drugs to Hide from Your Life, Inc. I went through a period of drug use and experimentation, and I stayed longer than I should have. I paid more than what I had, using drugs for pleasure, for partying, for days of being on top of the world, being creative, days of depression, days of joy, and nights of sadness.

As a kid growing up in a strict religious church, I almost never took any form of medication, not even an aspirin. I would dilute sodas because without the dilution, even sodas were too strong for me.

At that time, using drugs or taking medication was unthinkable! That would never be me. But while I was in college, I did eventually experiment with drugs. Several people I knew smoked marijuana, and while I was not a smoker because of asthma, I would indulge when I was around friends who smoked. When I moved to Los Angeles, I worked for a record company, and I was introduced to people who worked in the business and who used drugs frequently and were willing to share. This is where I met the self that I did not know existed. This was the self that thought I was OK, but the pain from my past came to visit me in various ways. Los Angeles is a great place to live. It is glamorous and exciting, especially when one is working in and or around the entertainment business.

Little by little, I became an occasional user of recreational drugs and prescription medication. I would go periods without using and then return to the drugs. Eventually, drugs became a common part of my life, just as common as getting up and taking a shower. When things were good, I would use, and when things were bad, I would use. There was this hole inside of me that others did not seem to notice. Was something wrong with my DNA? I just knew nothing fit. I was not present in my life, and I did not take good care of myself. I was always a day away from eviction or being fired. It did not look like it to some, but I was lost. I was hurting—being smart but living dumb. There was so much loneliness, so much pain of not feeling that I was good enough. Having survived rape and extreme abuse as a child, nothing really fit. I needed a new direction for my life. Drugs became my new best friend—a friend that did not disapprove of me, a friend that would make me feel better about myself. In the end, my friend turned on me and became cunning, baffling, and overpowering.

I considered myself "the dressed up professional addict". I did not look like an addict. I showed up for work, and I inspired and motivated those around me but when I was alone with my drugs, I knew the truth. I knew deep in my heart and soul that I was in serious trouble, but how could I get out of this place? Telling my secret was not something I wanted to do. Once I did not miss a beat. I looked good, smelled good, and excelled in my business. Eventually, my productivity started to fail. I could not get up and go to work, or I would call in with crazy excuses of why I could not come in. I started to isolate myself. "Me, my drugs and I."

I began to spiral downward—drugs came before rent. Eventually I was fired from my job, but I had drugs for consolation. I then started my own medical/science transcription business: The Write Word and even employed several part time workers. My business was the largest and most esteemed of its kind in the San Fernando Valley. One day, I could not show up for my own business. I let a lot of people down, but I just could not show up for my life any longer. A friend suggested I call Alcoholic Anonymous.

I started going to the meetings and got a sponsor. Things were looking up until I relapsed. I checked myself into an inpatient program. I did well and then relapsed again. I went to another in house program. I relapsed. But thank God, my sponsor continued to work with me. I continued to attend the 12 step meetings. I knew that by putting myself in the place where recovery was alive, would increase my chances for success. By attending meetings, working the program, being accountable, and taking directions from others who had sobriety, I experienced true recovery and peace of mind.

I now have over 20 years of sobriety. I regained all that I lost and more. I have a career as a social worker, mentor/coach, and I have been serving my community and empowering families for over 15 years. I am the mother of four children with special needs, an author and speaker.

Neecol Resnin, president and founder of Born for More, is a powerful motivator, teacher, and speaker. Neecol inspires and equips people to have faith in God and themselves and pursue their dreams no matter how outrageous they seem. She gives hope to the hopeless through her well-developed skills and strategies for success. An Ivy League grad with Masters in Business and Clinical Psychology, Neecol has 4 children and lives in Los Angeles.

www.BornForMore.com

The Agreement

By Barbara Starley

Success is an interesting word. Ask ten people for their definition of success and you are likely to get ten different answers. My "Rock Star" moment came as a result of a punishment imposed on my son which triggered a series of "Rock Star" opportunities for him as well.

It started out with a typical parent-teacher conference at the end of the first semester of my son's eighth grade year, his last year of Junior High at Edu-Prize Charter School. I loved visiting the classrooms, meeting Colton's teachers, and seeing all the projects on display. The halls were lined with posters and the classrooms were filled with incredible hands-on learning projects that the students had created throughout the semester. It was obvious that the kids worked hard and were engaged in what they were learning.

As we left that day, I was one proud mom! Colton's teachers loved having him in their classes and sang his praises as a model student, particularly when it came to anything that involved art. We talked about all that he was learning and how delighted we were that we had decided to stay at that school for junior high.

Then I asked him about a writing assignment that I saw on display in his history classroom, but I hadn't been able to find his. Colton explained that the assignment had been an "honors" project, and because he already had an "A" in the class, he had chosen not to do it. There was only one problem . . . we had an agreement that he would do all honors projects. He insisted that he saw absolutely no reason to do the honors project because he had a 104 percent in the class already, without doing it.

The whole purpose for honors projects, in Colton's mind, was to get extra credit in the class and potentially raise his grade. But in my mind, the honors projects were more about challenging the students and giving them a chance to go above and beyond what the average student would do. Besides. . . . we had an agreement that he would do all honors projects.

With that being said, I simply and (surprisingly) calmly told him that I expected him to complete the history project anyway—over Christmas break; and the real bummer was that he would get no school credit for the work he did. "I can't believe you're going to make me do that stupid project for no good reason," he said. But I had a good reason, we had an agreement and I expected him to honor it. The rest of the ride home was very quiet.

After some time of sulking in his room, Colton came to me with a proposition.

"That assignment that you're going to make me do was a writing assignment," he stated. "And it was for history class, right?" I agreed. "Well, if I write about history, can I write about anything I want?"

I was curious. "What did you have in mind?" I inquired.

"Well, I have an idea for a book. I already wrote the first chapter."

I looked up from the work I was doing. "What is it about?" I asked.

"The story takes place during World War I, which is what we are studying in History class."

"Okay," I said, "but you have to write every day during Christmas break, deal?"

And just like that, we had a deal. Colton got to write about what he wanted to write about and I still felt that he honored our agreement.

We spent most of the next three weeks at our cabin in the mountains, away from all the distractions at home. Every day, without being told, Colton would disappear into his room and type a chapter of his book. I loved it when he bounded down the stairs to tell me that his book was really taking shape, or that I was going to really like the chapter he had just written.

I could see the excitement on his face as Colton revealed only bits and pieces of the story each day. One day he came down and told me that I was not going to like the way one particular chapter ended; one of his characters had been killed. "This book takes place during World War I," he reminded me.

After three weeks, Colton had written twenty-one chapters. He put the final touches on his book over the next several weeks. We found a self-publishing company that would print-on-demand, and over the next year, I watched that book bless others, open doors, and give him opportunities that few kids enjoy.

Colton was invited to the retirement party of his third grade teacher. As we walked in, Mrs. Curtis greeted us and asked how his drawing was coming along, and then inquired, ". . . and what about writing? Are you writing, Colton? I always pegged you as a writer." Little did she know that in just a few moments, Colton would read a tribute to Mrs. Curtis and present her with a copy of his first book—dedicated to her!

When the World War I traveling museum came to Mesa, Arizona, Colton was invited to set up a table and sell his books to the hundreds of mostly elderly people waiting in line. It was heartwarming to watch him interact with many people who had stories of their own, of relatives, and friends they knew that fought in the war.

Colton's book received a Silver Medal by Moonbeam Children's Book Awards for "Best Book by a Young Author", and a local newspaper wrote a story about him and an 88-year-old author entitled "Never Too Young—or Old—to Write a Book".

But my real "Rock Star" moment came when Colton was invited to speak on stage at the Author 101 conference in Las Vegas. He had an audience of over 600 adults laughing, cheering, and applauding as he retold the story of our "agreement" and how the "relentless coaxing of his mother" was the beginning of his book, *Aura*.

Barbara Starley is a child of God and loves the Lord. She is a wife, mom, business owner, author, and speaker. Barbara is not your typical CPA. As a Certified QuickBooks® Pro Advisor, she has served hundreds of entrepreneurs and small business owners in the areas of QuickBooks® set-up, training, and troubleshooting. Her patient demeanor and in-depth knowledge is the perfect combination to turn confusion into confidence and help her clients become more successful and profitable.

www.BarbaraStarley.com

Stay Out of the Way of
a Mother with Grit

By Francine Tone

I was born in Japan, orphaned at age one, and adopted at age five. My adoptive father began molesting me shortly after. As an adult, I learned that my adoptive mother had shown all the signs of a battered woman, which finally explained why she could not protect me. By all accounts, I should have been an alcoholic, drug addict, prostitute, or prematurely dead. Yet, I survived and survived well. Somehow I garnered grit early in life. Grit made me a survivor. I survived the past and did something with myself. Grit got me through a failed marriage. Grit got me through 60 hours of hard labor to deliver a beautiful baby boy. Grit got me through law school at 33. Grit made me tough enough to become a professional skier at 51. Grit got me through cancer. I found a wonderful husband. And my son Kevin made it through the Air Force Academy. By 2002, I was living in Truckee, California, close to the ski resort and practicing law on my own terms. Life was really good. Then my world shattered.

On July 29, 2002, over 7000 miles away in New Zealand, my 24-year old Air Force pilot son was found unconscious on a ski run. When I received the call at 4:00 PM California time, still July 28, 2002, he was on a helicopter en route to a hospital in New Zealand and I didn't know if he was dead or alive. By the end of the day, I learned he was alive, but in a coma having suffered a severe traumatic brain injury.

I rushed to New Zealand. When I arrived, the doctors told me to prepare myself because my son would be a vegetable for the rest of his life. They showed me the results of the brain scan. I stared at the images with confusion because I saw nothing wrong until the doctors told me that white meant brain cells had been destroyed. The entire image was white. They explained that when blood touches a brain cell, it kills the brain cell. The white meant there had been massive bleeding on the brain.

I sat with my son, holding his hand, every day for three weeks in that hospital, leaving only to sleep for 6 hours every two days. I spoke to him despite his comatose state, and I saw changes every day. I saw him coming out of his coma little by little. Every time I reported a change, a doctor would repeat the prognosis: he will be a vegetable for the rest of his life. Finally, I turned to a doctor and told him, "Duly noted. If my son hasn't changed in two years, I'll consider accepting the prognosis. But not now!"

Eventually we ended up in Palo Alto, at the premier brain injury/stroke rehabilitation center. Even there, I was told repeatedly to lower my expectations and resolve myself to my son living at home for the rest of his life, possibly working at a small local store. I know I frustrated doctors and nurses because I scoffed at their low expectations. I lived with the mantra that NOW was not the time to lower expectations.

From the moment I began arranging my trip to New Zealand, my husband and I began reading every book, article, snippet about the brain that had been published in the past five years, and there were a lot of them. I scoured the internet looking for anything authoritative and useful. Funny thing about the brain, no one really knows that much about it. The good news was, everyone agreed every brain injury was different and that one should be cautious about over-generalizing a particular brain injury. This meant I could justify my overly-positive attitude and absolute resolve that my son was going to recover; a pox on anyone who said otherwise. This meant that whatever approach I took, if it didn't hurt him, it could help him.

One thing I did figure out, or so I think I figured out, was that Kevin had to grow up again. In the first round, he had been given opportunities, as with any child in a middle class home. He was allowed to play; he went to school; he watched TV; he played video games; he sat around "bored" sometimes; he associated with friends and family. After the brain injury, he had to "grow up" all over again. But this time, he didn't have the luxury of spreading out his growing up over 24 years. He had to do it now and quickly so he could move on with his life. This meant that his exposure to learning had to be systematic and calculated. So I set out to create a systematic approach to his brain development, which began unknowingly while still in New Zealand.

In New Zealand, a reflexologist offered her services and she performed reflexology on the meridians associated with the brain. The doctors said it wouldn't hurt, so we did it. The reflexologist taught me about homeopathic cures. The doctors told me I could do anything that didn't hurt, so I did. By the time we returned to California, I had learned more and learned that I could be more systematic in my approach. I questioned everything anyone told me, researched it, and put into practice activities designed to stimulate the brain and allow for healing. When I found brain training programs (which were just starting to come out), I got them for Kevin. Anything that stimulated the brain, based on what I had been learning, might help and couldn't hurt. I simulated 24 years of learning into a shorter span of time, starting with using a fork and tying his shoes.

It has now been 14 years since the accident. Kevin has since left the Air Force. After a brain injury, he wasn't going to fly a plane, much less a fighter jet, again. He has obtained his Master's Degree in World Peace and Conflict Resolution. He is a strategic military planner for the Air Force in Europe, living alone in Europe. He travels the world for business and pleasure. He was just home for the holidays. He is in top physical shape with rock hard abs. If you met him today, you'd see no clue what he's gone through. At long-term follow ups, the doctors are stunned at his recovery.

Grit got me through this. And I'm thankful that Kevin has managed to develop grit. I'm convinced he too, can get through anything.

Life is, again, really good.

Francine Tone is a lawyer, professional athlete, professional speaker, and #1 bestselling author. Aside from being the managing partner of her law firm Tone & Tone, she helps women and girls confidently and successfully unlock their power and dreams to transform their lives personally and in business.

www.FrancineTone.com

How to Tip the Scales in Your Favor and Create Harmony in Your Business Life

By Tesy Ward

Congratulations, you've chosen to live the life of an Entrepreneur! Welcome to the ranks of brave souls who prefer freedom, autonomy, and unbridled earning potential over the status quo. Entrepreneurship is a unique way of life, which creates second chances, allowing those who are disenfranchised from more traditional modes of employment, to become masters of their own destiny. It is a game changer for those otherwise cut off from climbing the traditional corporate ladder due to negative life experiences, mental/physical health challenges, and a lack of opportunity. It has the capacity to rally communities and galvanize its constituents around a common goal, which yields exponential benefits. It is a way for women and young adults to become empowered, self-sustaining business people, who are capable of challenging and changing traditional societal roles.

For me, there's no better way of life. Yes, a way of life! Being an Entrepreneur is a full time, all consuming, pursuit. It requires boldness, courage, and a tremendous amount of faith in one's own abilities.

That said, the road to success is not without challenges and pitfalls. Throughout my Entrepreneurial journey, I've had more than my share of roadblocks, stumbles, and full on disasters! Problems, which at the time seemed insurmountable, crumbled before me as long as I could manage to do one thing . . . BREATHE. The simple process of coming to a full stop, taking a few deep breaths in order to recenter myself, harness my talents, experience, and wisdom, to use for my advantage, has never failed to rescue me from failure.

Rather than regale you with Rock and Roll stories of my life in music, I wish to share 5 tenets, which I've learned throughout a lifetime of Entrepreneurship. They are my foundation and the secret to my long-lasting success. May they help you live your dreams and reach the stars. Rock On!

1. Do Not Produce or Develop Anything until You Sell It First!

Many aspiring Entrepreneurs disregard this principle and find themselves failing prior to their launch. Keep your start-up costs low and channel your resources into ascertaining if your vision is something which people are actually willing to purchase, preferably, on an ongoing basis. As you query your potential customer base, be sure to keep your own ego in check. It is critical to listen to, and learn from, your customer's criticism and suggestions. Market Intelligence is vital to successful sales, promotion, and distribution. Your customers will validate and refine your ideas and ensure your success, if you allow them to!

2. Use Social Media to Shine, Not Just to Sell.

Customers love to see "the backstory" of their favorite brands, products, and the people who create them. Social Media outlets give an opportunity to share who you really are and what passions drive you to do what you do. Giving your customers a chance to go "back stage" and observe your process is key to building brand loyalty. Do not bash them over the head with a sales pitch, no matter how tempting it may be to close the sale. People buy from those they have a kinship with. Be real, be human, be accessible, and the sales will happen organically. The loyalty you build along the way will sustain both your customer and your business. Products and services are a dime a dozen. People want to experience a brand, and feel that they are an intricate part of its creation and growth.

3. Stay on Top of the World, or at Least Your Little Piece of It.

As an Entrepreneur, there is never time to rest on your laurels. In addition to providing customers with best-in-class products, savvy Entrepreneurs seek to become data-centric enterprises. It's a wise businessperson who not only collects data, but deeply analyzes it and utilizes the results to provide their business with a unique competitive edge, thereby distancing their competition and ensuring market domination. Accurate, timely, pertinent information is the lifeblood of a successful venture. Smart Entrepreneurs invest the time and resources to ascertain and maintain their relevance in the marketplace.

4. Closing Your First Sales.

This is the moment you have been waiting for, finally bringing a product or service to market, then basking in the glow as the funds roll in from the first sales. So, are you a success? Well, maybe, but quite possibly, not. This is an area where many Entrepreneurs fail to hit the mark. At first blush, one might believe any cash is good cash, correct? Especially if you have Venture Capitalists and Investors breathing down your neck to make sales and produce income. WRONG! If your only sales are to friends, family, and peer groups, you are depriving yourself of vital information. Did these "customers" purchase your product because of its tremendous value and unique qualities? Or, was their purchase motivated by an inflated sense of loyalty, love, obligation, or heaven forbid . . . pity? I'm not suggesting you forgo these sales, but do be sure you have an overabundance of arm's-length transactions, so you can glean critical, much needed data from them. These buyers are essential to your initial and long-term success. When assessed properly, these customers can provide insight and feedback which allows you to not only fine tune your product or service, but your sales methods as well. Feedback of this type is invaluable, as it allows you to develop a unique bond with your customer base, resulting in long term loyalty, repeat sales, and mutual transaction satisfaction.

5. Mentorship and Philanthropy

By joining the ranks of Entrepreneurship, you take an unwritten, unspoken oath to foster the dreams and aspirations of those who will follow in your Entrepreneurial footsteps. You are duty bound to offer guidance, knowledge, and the fruits of your mistakes as well as your successes.

As you enjoy your prosperity, be ever mindful that there are many who need your support. Sometimes it might be a shoulder to cry on, sometimes it might be a need for sage business advice. Often times, it will be a need, which can only be satiated by financial assistance. Be the first to meet these needs for those who most require it. There is no greater reward that Entrepreneurship, or life, can bestow upon you.

In closing, the true heart of Entrepreneurship lies in the realization that financial gain is not the only goal. Lasting success resides in how we choose to pursue our goals, despite what we do or do not have, the lessons we learn along the way, and the people we positively impact and influence throughout our journey.

Tesy Ward is a successful Businesswoman and Philanthropist, who is known for her ability to identify, cultivate, and bring to market "hidden gems" within the music and entertainment industries. Her unique approach to business emanates from a lifetime of experience as a Singer, Lyricist, and Developer of musical talent.

www.TesyWard.com

"Photography—My Cure for a Bad Memory"

By Lori Zapata

A year ago, I was broken. The man I was married to for over 17 years, my best friend, the man who I thought was the love of my life, decided he didn't love me anymore. I was fighting cancer at the time and yet that was the least of my health concerns. In addition to Ovarian Cancer, I had a debilitating health condition that caused excruciating pain 24/7, and now my best friend was gone and I was alone. I was always a strong woman but so much had happened. It caught up with me and I was truly broken.

In total disbelief, I would wonder, how did I get here, how did it come to this? The past few years had been a struggle with one crisis after another. I had been living with severe chronic pain for years, lost a six figure job that I loved, and then suddenly lost my mom. My husband was in a car accident shortly after my mom's death and was out of work for a year. Next, I was diagnosed with ovarian cancer and had surgery to remove a tumor the size of an eggplant. Following that, I had to make life changing treatment decisions on how to proceed post-surgery. With the stress of all that was happening, my chronic pain condition, which of course worsens with stress, was unbearable. As if all this wasn't enough, my husband then lost his job, and with it, my health insurance. I knew our marriage was stressed to its limits. What marriage wouldn't be? However, we were best friends, soul mates, and we were committed. That was never in question for me. I believed with all my heart that we would get through this together. I was wrong.

No one can possibly know what it is like to live with chronic debilitating pain, except those that do. I was in pain every day from Hidradenitis Suppurativa, a rare, long term, and debilitating condition. I suffered for years and years with no relief in sight. Most people never knew. I showed up for life every day with a smile and kept the pain hidden. Hidden from everyone but my husband, though even he didn't know how bad I really felt. I failed to see the effect my pain had on our relationship. I thought I could lean on him and count on him. Had the roles been reversed, I would have been there for him. That is who I am. Situations in our past prove that. However, he was not Me, and he left.

Physically and emotionally broken, I found comfort in a saying, ***"Don't feel sad over someone who gave up on you . . . feel sorry for them because they gave up on someone that would have never given up on them."*** This was one of the first steps that helped me realize that despite how bad I felt, I actually liked who I was. I was honest, loyal, dedicated, and hard working. I was smart, and I was strong and maybe most important of all, I realized, I was worthy. Worthy of help if I wasn't feeling well, and worthy of love without conditions.

Through the pain and the loss, I had been trying to start my own photography business. With all that was going on, why then? Well there is nothing like a life-threatening disease to make you realize life is precious and short and why not try to make a living, and a life, doing something you love. Photography was always a passion for me and I was determined to make it work.

I had been taking pictures for years, but needed to head back to school to master digital photography. My business grew slowly, but it was a steady growth and things improved each week, and each month. One thing I love about photography is the many directions you can take. Many photographers choose to specialize in one area, I prefer to mix it up. My business card says it all, "I Shoot Things", weddings, events, sports, concerts, portraits, and just about anything. I find it keeps me fresh and excited about what I am shooting.

A friend of mine landed a concert shoot for me with a singer songwriter that I had admired for years. If you asked me who my favorite singer was at anytime, I would have told you Linda Eder. She won Star Search in 1980 and went on to Broadway and continues performing concerts today. I was always a big fan. Long story short, I met Linda and after the second show I shot for her, she told me she wanted to use my photographs for her upcoming CD. This was truly a dream come true. Not only did my photographs end up on Linda Eder's CD "Linda Live", but they were also published in the Chicago Tribune. As a photographer, it is a benchmark of success to be published. I had been published in the New York Hockey Journal, which was an honor, but the Chicago Tribune? Well that was truly a highlight of my career. That and having my photographs on my idol's CD, I knew then that I made it. I was a professional photographer.

Today, I am no longer broken. I am currently cancer free and working my way toward that five-year cancer free goal. With regard to my chronic pain, an amazing resident doctor tried something experimental and I am pain-free most days. I am healing and I am happy. My life is changing and I look forward to the adventures that lie ahead. Starting over later in life is not easy, however, I came through a lot and know I can face whatever life puts in front of me. It helps to have two amazing sons that are always looking out for their mom.

So, am I a woman who rocks? The answer now is easy . . . "Hell Yes!"

Lori Zapata is a Nikon Professional Photographer, moment-chaser, memory-keeper, from New York. Her passion and skill for photography has been seen in the Chicago Tribune, The New York Hockey Journal, and other publications. Lori enjoys shooting everything from Weddings to Hockey to Rock Stars.

www.LoriZapata.com

For more books and products by
Craig & Natasha Duswalt please visit
www.CraigDuswalt.com/online-store